13th International Conference on Computational Semantics (IWCS 2019)

Student Papers

Gothenburg, Sweden
23-27 May 2019

ISBN: 978-1-5108-8762-6

Printed from e-media with permission by:

Curran Associates, Inc.
57 Morehouse Lane
Red Hook, NY 12571

Some format issues inherent in the e-media version may also appear in this print version.

Printed by Curran Associates, Inc. (2019)

For permission requests, please contact the Association for Computational Linguistics at the address below.

Association for Computational Linguistics
209 N. Eighth Street
Stroudsburg, Pennsylvania 18360

Phone: 1-570-476-8006
Fax: 1-570-476-0860

acl@aclweb.org

Additional copies of this publication are available from:

Curran Associates, Inc.
57 Morehouse Lane
Red Hook, NY 12571 USA
Phone: 845-758-0400
Fax: 845-758-2633
Email: curran@proceedings.com
Web: www.proceedings.com

IWCS 2019

Proceedings of the 13th International Conference on Computational Semantics - Student Papers

23–27 May, 2019

University of Gothenburg

Gothenburg, Sweden

Introduction

Welcome to the 13th edition of the International Conference on Computational Semantics (IWCS 2019) in Gothenburg. The aim of IWCS is to bring together researchers interested in any aspects of the annotation, representation and computation of meaning in natural language, whether this is from a lexical or structural semantic perspective. It embraces both symbolic and machine learning approaches to computational semantics, and everything in between. This is reflected in the themes of the sessions which take place over full 3 days. The programme starts with formal and grammatical approaches to the representation and computation of meaning, interaction of these approaches with distributional approaches, explore the issues related to entailment, semantic relations and frames, and unsupervised learning of word embeddings and semantic representations, including those that involve information from other modalities such as images. Overall, the papers capture a good overview of different angles from which the computational approach to natural language semantics can be studied.

The talks of our three keynote speakers also reflect these themes. The work of Mehrnoosh Sadrzadeh focuses on combination categorial grammars with word- and sentence embeddings for disambiguation of sentences with VP ellipsis. The work of Ellie Pavlick focuses on the evaluation of the state-of-the art data-driven models of language for what they "understand" in terms of inference and what is their internal structure. Finally, the work of Raffaella Bernardi focuses on conversational agents that learn grounded language in visual information through interactions with other agents. We are delighted they have accepted our invitation and we are looking forward to their talks.

In total, we accepted 25 long papers (51% of submissions), 10 short papers (44% of submissions) and 7 student papers (54% of submissions) following the recommendations of our peer reviewers. Each paper was reviewed by three experts. We are extremely grateful to the Programme Committee members for their detailed and helpful reviews. The long and student papers will be presented either as talks or posters, while short papers will be presented as posters. Overall, there are 7 sessions of talks and 2 poster sessions (introduced by short lighting talks) which we organised according to the progression of the themes over 3 days, starting each day with a keynote talk. The sessions are organised in a way to allow plenty of time in between to allow participants to initiate discussions over a Swedish *fika*.

To encourage a broader participation of students we organised a student track where the papers have undergone the same quality review as long papers but at the same time the reviewers were instructed to provide comments that are beneficial to their authors to develop their work. To this end we also awarded a Best Student Paper Award.

The conference is preceded by 5 workshops on semantic annotation, meaning relations, types and frames, vector semantics and dialogue, and on interactions between natural language processing and theoretical computer science. In addition to the workshops, this year there is also a shared task on semantic parsing. The workshops and the shared task will take place over the two days preceding the conference.

There will be two social events. A reception which is sponsored by the City of Gothenburg will be opened by the Lord Mayor of Gothenburg and will take place on the evening of the second day of the workshops and before the main conference. A conference dinner will take place in Liseberg Amusement Park where participants will also get a chance to try some of their attractions.

IWCS 2019 has received general financial support (covering over a half of the costs) from the Centre for Linguistics Theory and Studies in Probability (CLASP) which in turn is financed by a grant from the Swedish Research Council (VR project 2014-39) and University of Gothenburg. CLASP also hosts the event. We are also grateful to the Masters Programme in Language Technology (MLT) at the University of Gothenburg, Talkamatic AB and the City of Gothenburg for their financial support.

We very much hope that you will have an enjoyable and inspiring time!

Simon Dobnik, Stergios Chatzikyriakidis, and Vera Demberg

Gothenburg & Saarbrücken

May 2019

Organisers:

Local Chairs: Stergios Chatzikyriakidis and Simon Dobnik
Program Chairs: Stergios Chatzikyriakidis, Vera Demberg, and Simon Dobnik
Workshops Chair: Asad Sayeed
Student Track Chairs: Vlad Maraev and Chatrine Qwaider
Sponsorships Chair: Staffan Larsson

Program Committee:

Lasha Abzianidze, Laura Aina, Maxime Amblard, Krasimir Angelov, Emily M. Bender, Raffaella Bernardi, Jean-Philippe Bernardy , Rasmus Blanck, Gemma Boleda, Alessandro Bondielli, Lars Borin, Johan Bos, Ellen Breitholtz, Harry Bunt, Aljoscha Burchardt, Nicoletta Calzolari, Emmanuele Chersoni, Philipp Cimiano, Stephen Clark, Robin Cooper, Philippe de Groote, Vera Demberg, Simon Dobnik, Devdatt Dubhashi, Katrin Erk, Arash Eshghi, Raquel Fernández, Jonathan Ginzburg, Matthew Gotham, Eleni Gregoromichelaki, Justyna Grudzinska, Gözde Gül Şahin, Iryna Gurevych , Dag Haug, Aurelie Herbelot, Julian Hough, Christine Howes, Elisabetta Jezek, Richard Johansson, Alexandre Kabbach, Lauri Karttunen, Ruth Kempson, Mathieu Lafourcade, Gabriella Lapesa, Shalom Lappin, Staffan Larsson, Gianluca Lebani, Kiyong Lee, Alessandro Lenci, Martha Lewis, Maria Liakata, Sharid Loáiciga, Zhaohui Luo, Moritz Maria, Aleksandre Maskharashvili, Stephen Mcgregor, Louise McNally, Bruno Mery, Mehdi Mirzapour, Richard Moot, Alessandro Moschitti, Larry Moss, Diarmuid O Seaghdha, Sebastian Pado, Ludovica Pannitto, Ivandre Paraboni, Lucia C. Passaro, Sandro Pezzelle, Manfred Pinkal, Paul Piwek, Massimo Poesio, Sylvain Pogodalla, Christopher Potts, Stephen Pulman, Matthew Purver, James Pustejovsky, Alessandro Raganato, Giulia Rambelli, Allan Ramsay, Aarne Ranta, Christian Retoré, Martin Riedl, Roland Roller, Mehrnoosh Sadrzadeh, Asad Sayeed, Tatjana Scheffler, Sabine Schulte Im Walde, Marco S. G. Senaldi, Manfred Stede, Matthew Stone, Allan Third, Kees Van Deemter, Eva Maria Vecchi, Carl Vogel, Ivan Vulić, Bonnie Webber, Roberto Zamparelli

Invited Speakers:

Mehrnoosh Sadrzadeh, Queen Mary, University of London
Ellie Pavlick, Brown University
Raffaella Bernardi, University of Trento

Table of Contents

A Dynamic Semantics for Causal Counterfactuals

Kenneth Lai
Department of Computer Science
Brandeis University
Waltham, MA 02453
klai12@brandeis.edu

James Pustejovsky
Department of Computer Science
Brandeis University
Waltham, MA 02453
jamesp@brandeis.edu

Abstract

Under the standard approach to counterfactuals, to determine the meaning of a counterfactual sentence, we consider the "closest" possible world(s) where the antecedent is true, and evaluate the consequent. Building on the standard approach, some researchers have found that the set of worlds to be considered is dependent on context; it evolves with the discourse. Others have focused on how to define the "distance" between possible worlds, using ideas from causal modeling. This paper integrates the two ideas. We present a semantics for counterfactuals that uses a distance measure based on causal laws, that can also change over time. We show how our semantics can be implemented in the Haskell programming language.

1 Introduction and background

The problem of modeling counterfactual statements and situations has drawn much attention, in computer science, linguistics, and other disciplines. In addition to its intrinsic interest, counterfactual reasoning is important for artificial intelligence systems to be able to handle novel situations (Pearl and Mackenzie, 2018).

The classic approach to counterfactuals in linguistics and philosophy is based on a possible-worlds semantics (Lewis, 1973; Stalnaker, 1968; Kratzer, 1981). To evaluate a counterfactual, we examine a possible world where the antecedent is true, and evaluate the consequent. For example, let us consider the following classic example from Lewis (1973):

(1) If kangaroos had no tails, they would topple over.

In the actual world, kangaroos have tails, but we can think of a possible world in which they do not, and consider whether they topple over in that world. However, not all possible worlds should be considered. We can consider a world in which kangaroos have no tails, but use crutches, and perhaps they would not topple over in that world. But in the actual world, kangaroos do not use crutches, so why should we consider those worlds in which they do? We therefore only consider the "closest" possible worlds to the actual world, according to some distance metric or ordering of worlds.

Formally, we have an accessibility relation R, such that $R(w, w')$ is true if and only if w' is sufficiently similar to w. This defines for each world w a context, or *modal horizon*, consisting of those worlds w' such that $R(w, w')$ (von Fintel, 2001). A counterfactual $\phi > \psi$ is true in a world if and only if in all the worlds in the modal horizon where ϕ is true, ψ is true.

Von Fintel (2001) provides evidence that this context changes over time, by considering sequences of counterfactuals. Briefly, if there are no worlds in the modal horizon where the antecedent ϕ is true, the modal horizon expands until it includes those ϕ-worlds most similar to the current world. However, after the counterfactual has been evaluated, the accessibility relation does not revert to its previous state. For example, consider the following sequence of counterfactuals (a *Lewis-Sobel sequence*):

(2) If kangaroos had no tails, they would topple over.
If kangaroos had no tails but used crutches, they would not topple over.

In the closest possible worlds in which kangaroos have no tails, they do not use crutches, and do topple over. However, in the closest worlds in which kangaroos both have no tails and use crutches, they do not topple over. The above sequence makes sense. But the next sequence of counterfactuals, with the order of the sentences reversed (a *reverse Sobel sequence*), is semantically infelicitous:

(3) If kangaroos had no tails but used crutches, they would not topple over.
#If kangaroos had no tails, they would topple over.

The first sentence expands the modal horizon to include worlds in which kangaroos have no tails and use crutches. Once we have introduced worlds in which kangaroos use crutches, we cannot subsequently forget about them when thinking of worlds where they have no tails. Therefore, when evaluating the second sentence, we must consider all worlds in the modal horizon where kangaroos have no tails, including both worlds in which they do and those in which they do not use crutches. In some of these worlds, they topple over, and in others, they do not.

In the classic possible-worlds approach to counterfactuals, the notion of distance or similarity between worlds is deliberately left underspecified. However, a computational implementation of counterfactuals must specify the distance metric to be used. Let us consider a possible world to be characterized by the "facts" true in that world (Kratzer, 1981). Given two worlds that differ from the actual world in the same number of facts, which one is closer? Pollock (1976) suggests that "subjunctive generalizations" are more important than other facts, while Kratzer (1981) suggests that certain facts should be "lumped" together. For example, if one looks in a mirror, one would expect to see their reflection, even if it is not currently visible (because they are not currently looking in the mirror). In other words, the facts "one looks in a mirror" and "one sees their reflection" should be lumped together: if the truth value of one fact changes, the truth of the other should change as well.

A related idea from Pearl (2000) is that the distances between worlds rely on the notion of cause and effect. Specifically, worlds that differ in their causal laws are more distant than worlds whose laws are the same. If we say that looking in a mirror causes one to see their reflection, then among worlds where one looks in the mirror, those in which they see their reflection are closer to the actual world than those where they do not.

Pearl formulates causal laws in terms of structural equations. An equation $a = f(b)$ denotes that, in a particular world, the value of a is dependent on the value of b. This allows us to reason about what the value of a would have been, if the value of b had been different. The set of structural equations, together with an enumeration of the variables, defines a causal model. While Pearl's framework cannot model all possible counterfactual sentences, others have extended the causal modeling approach to different types of counterfactuals (Briggs, 2012).

Causal modeling approaches to counterfactuals make use of interventions: changes in the causal model (Pearl, 2000). Specifically, to evaluate a counterfactual sentence, change the underlying model to make the antecedent true, and allow the change to propagate through the model. Then evaluate the consequent with respect to the new model. Briggs (2012), making connections between causal modeling and possible-worlds approaches, identifies causal models with possible worlds. Applying an intervention then corresponds to selecting the closest possible world where the antecedent is true.

In this paper, we present a semantics for counterfactual sentences that integrates causal reasoning with a dynamic semantics, such as that of Groenendijk and Stokhof (1991). Causal reasoning allows us to give an exact specification of the vague notion of "distance" between worlds, while a dynamic semantics allows us to analyze how the meaning of counterfactuals changes with context. The key idea connecting these two approaches is that causal laws can be encoded in an accessibility relation, and therefore a change in context is equivalent to an intervention in the causal model. We can formalize this using ideas from Alternating-time Temporal Logic with Intentions (ATL+I), a logic for strategic reasoning (Jamroga et al., 2005). We also present a computational implementation of our semantics in the Haskell programming language, available at `https://github.com/klai12/dscc`.

2 Causal models and concurrent game structures

Our implementation is based on *concurrent game structures*, introduced by Alur et al. (2002) as an extension of Kripke structures to open (multi-agent) systems. A Kripke structure contains a set of possible worlds, a set of propositions, and a labeling function from worlds to sets of propositions true in those worlds (Kripke, 1963). Concurrent game structures add a set of players, where each player has, for each possible world, a non-empty set of moves available at that world. The transitions available from some world are determined by the moves taken by each player at that world.

We can formally assign types to the above components as follows. We take worlds, propositions, players, and moves to be primitive types `World`, `Prop`, `Player`, and `Move`, respectively. It will be convenient to also define a type `Vector` for move vectors, i.e., which move is taken by each player, as `[(Player, Move)]`. A concurrent game structure then consists of the following six components:

- A set A of players, of type `[Player]`;
- A set W of worlds, of type `[World]`;
- A set P of propositions, of type `[Prop]`;
- A labeling function L, of type `World -> [Prop]`;
- A move function D, of type `Player -> World -> [Move]`;
- A transition function δ, of type `World -> Vector -> World`.

We now introduce the notion of a *strategy*. We adopt the definition in (Jamroga et al., 2005), as a function that, for a given player, maps each world to a non-empty subset of the moves available to that player at that world. Strategies therefore have type `World -> [Move]`. We can then define a "strategy function" σ as a non-empty subset of the move function, with type `Player -> Strategy` (or equivalently `Player -> World -> [Move]`), that specifies a strategy for each player. In ATL+I, because the strategies employed by each player restrict the set of moves from which the player will choose, and the transitions allowed from a world depend on the moves made by each player, the strategy function therefore determines which transitions are allowed. The set of allowed transitions, in turn, forms an accessibility relation that depends on the strategies used by each player.

To return to the setting of counterfactuals, we recall that in a dynamic semantics, the accessibility relation (or modal horizon) changes over time. Furthermore, using a causal modeling approach, the change in the accessibility relation is determined by an intervention in a causal model. Our proposal is to identify variables in a causal model with players in a concurrent game structure. Then we can use the strategy for a player to encode the structural equation for that variable, such that a change in strategy corresponds to an intervention in the causal model.

2.1 Example: Kangaroos, tails, and crutches

As an illustrative example, we will again consider the case of the kangaroos. Let us assume that kangaroos will topple over if and only if they have no tails and they do not use crutches; otherwise they will stay upright. Let Q, R, and S be Boolean variables corresponding to whether kangaroos have tails, use crutches, and topple over, respectively. Then we can write the structural equation $S = \neg Q \wedge \neg R$ to encode this causal law.

Now we can represent our scenario as a concurrent game structure. First, the set of players in our model is $A = \{Q, R, S\}$. Each variable in the causal model is a player in the concurrent game structure. Note that despite the use of the term "player", the players in our model are not agents, or even entities, for that matter; there are no players corresponding to "kangaroos", "tails", or "crutches".

Next we consider the space of possible worlds. We will introduce a possible world for each possible combination of moves the players can make. We will discuss the meanings of the different moves each player can make below; for now, we will say that players Q and R have two moves each (which we will call 0 and 1), and S has three moves (which we will call 0, 1, and x). Therefore, there are $2 \times 2 \times 3 = 12$ possible worlds in our concurrent game structure. We will also say that each player has the same set of available moves at each world; i.e., for all worlds w, the move function D is specified by $D(Q, w) = D(R, w) = \{0, 1\}$, and $D(S, w) = \{0, 1, x\}$. We will label the possible worlds according to the moves made by each player to arrive at that world; e.g., w_{10x} is the possible world that results when Q makes move 1, R makes move 0, and S makes move x. The combination $\{(Q, 1), (R, 0), (S, x)\}$ is then a move vector, and therefore we know that for all worlds w, the transition function $\delta(w, \{(Q, 1), (R, 0), (S, x)\}) = w_{10x}$. We can calculate the other values of the transition function in the same way.

We have specified the possible moves for each player at each world, but what do the moves mean? Although our players are not agents in the conventional sense, we can nevertheless think of them as being able to "set" their own values. For all players, then, the move 0 sets its value to 0 in the next world, while 1 sets its value to 1.

The above moves are sufficient for those variables that are exogenous, i.e., those whose values are not dependent on the values of any other variables. In our scenario, Q and R are exogenous variables. For an endogenous variable such as S, whose value is dependent on the values of Q and R, it is not possible to represent the causal law governing S, only using some combination of moves 0 and 1. The reason is because the value of S in the next world is dependent on the values of Q and R in the next world, not the current world. For endogenous variables, therefore, we introduce a third move x, which sets the value of the endogenous variable according to its structural equation. For example, the move x for player S sets the value of S in the next world to be equal to $\neg Q \wedge \neg R$. In summary, exogenous variables have two moves 0 and 1, while endogenous variables have a third move x.

The initial set of propositions is $P = \{q, r, s\}$. Our propositions correspond to valuations of each of the variables; e.g., q is true in those worlds where the value of Q is 1, etc. Where necessary, the values of endogenous variables can be calculated using their structural equations. For example, the value of S in w_{10x} is $\neg 1 \wedge \neg 0 = 0 \wedge 1 = 0$. The labeling function is then straightforward to calculate: $L(w_{000}) = \varnothing$, $L(w_{10x}) = \{q\}$, etc.

Finally, we must specify our initial conditions: the initial strategies of each player. For player S, the strategy is to enforce the causal law $S = \neg Q \wedge \neg R$ at each world. Therefore the strategy for S is simply $\lambda w.x$: at all worlds w, make move x.

As for players Q and R, because they are exogenous variables, they do not have structural equations in Pearl's causal models (Pearl, 2000). However, we do not want to say that they have no strategies. As previously mentioned, when evaluating a counterfactual sentence, we only want to consider those worlds that are closest to the actual world. But in ATL+I, having no strategy means placing no restrictions on which worlds are accessible from the actual world (Jamroga et al., 2005). Intuitively, given a world with some value of Q, worlds with the same value of Q can be considered closer to that world than worlds with the opposite value, all else being equal. Therefore, one possible strategy is to keep the value of Q the same:

$$\sigma(Q) = \lambda w. \begin{cases} 1, & q \in L(w) \\ 0, & \text{otherwise} \end{cases}$$

The strategy for R can be similarly specified.

3 The dynamics of causal counterfactuals

Now we can describe the evaluation of counterfactual sentences in our framework. We translate sentences into formulas of type `Form`. In addition to the formulas of propositional and basic modal logic, we also include the formula scheme `Str a strategy phi`; these correspond to ATL+I sentences $(\mathbf{str}_a \sigma_a)\phi$. In ATL+I, it is the evaluation of **str**-formulas in which changes of strategy occur; in our framework, counterfactual sentences are translated into **str**-formulas for evaluation.

Formulas must of course be evaluated relative to some model. In addition, in a dynamic semantics, we must also keep track of the context. To do this, we make use of Haskell's state monad. We define the type `Model` of our states as a record type, that includes the current strategy function, as well as four components of our concurrent game structure: the sets of players and worlds, and the labeling and transition functions. Because of how we constructed our concurrent game structures above, the set of propositions and the move function can be inferred from the other components.

For a given function (and context), our model checker returns the set of possible worlds where the formula is true. As such, our main function, `check`, has type `Form -> State Model [World]`. The model checker is based heavily on that in (Jamroga et al., 2005) for ATL+I, which itself is derived from the model checker for ATL in (Alur et al., 2002). Propositions are checked using the labeling function, and formulas of propositional logic follow via the usual set-theoretic operations. The checking of modal formulas makes use of a pre-image function, which, given a set of possible worlds, returns the set of worlds that can access any of those worlds. Then, for example, to check a formula $\Diamond\phi$, we first find the set of worlds where ϕ is true, and then calculate the set of worlds such that the ϕ-worlds are accessible.

Finally, to check **str**-formulas, we introduce a `revise` function. This is the mechanism by which causal interventions are modeled. Formally, let σ be the current strategy for player a, and σ' be a's new strategy. Then we can say that $\texttt{revise}(a, \sigma') = \{\sigma \cup \sigma'\}$.

We should note that our `revise` function differs from that of Jamroga et al. (2005). Whereas changes of strategy in ATL+I involve replacement of the player's previous strategy, our `revise` function simply add the moves from σ' to a's previous strategy. We recall that in von Fintel's dynamic account of counterfactuals, the accessibility relation (modal horizon) expands but does not contract. In other words, all worlds accessible from a given world before an update to the model, remain accessible afterwards.

Returning to the kangaroos, we can now see the difference in the evaluation of the Lewis-Sobel sequence in (2) and the reverse Sobel sequence in (3). We will use the propositions q, r, and s as before, to represent kangaroos having tails, using crutches, and toppling over, respectively. In evaluating the sentence "If kangaroos had no tails, they would topple over" under the causal modeling approach, we apply an intervention in the model to set $Q = 0$. This corresponds to a strategy for Q to go to a world where $\neg q$ is true; i.e., $\lambda w.0$. Then, following von Fintel (2001), we check whether in all accessible worlds where $\neg q$ is true, s is also true; this is the strict conditional $\Box(\neg q \to s)$. Therefore, the formula we want to evaluate is $(\mathbf{str}_Q(\lambda w.0))\Box(\neg q \to s)$.

Similarly, when we evaluate the sentence "If kangaroos had no tails but used crutches, they would not topple over", we want to expand our modal horizon to include worlds where $\neg q$ and r are both true. This involves changes in strategy by both Q and R; Q to set $Q = 0$, R to set $R = 1$. The formula to be evaluated must therefore include both an $(\mathbf{str}_Q(\lambda w.0))$ term and an $(\mathbf{str}_R(\lambda w.1))$ term. Then, since we want to check the truth of $\neg s$ in those accessible worlds where both $\neg q$ and r are true, our formula is $(\mathbf{str}_Q(\lambda w.0))(\mathbf{str}_R(\lambda w.1))\Box((\neg q \wedge r) \to \neg s)$.

Suppose that starting from our initial conditions, the sentence "If kangaroos had no tails, they would topple over" is uttered. We first update the strategy function for Q, to add the move 0 to Q's initial strategy. This has no effect in worlds where $Q = 0$, as the default strategy for Q is to keep its value the same. However, in worlds where $Q = 1$, Q now has two moves consistent with its new strategy, 0 and 1. Now, using the updated accessibility relation, we evaluate the formula $\Box(\neg q \to s)$. Every world now has an accessible $\neg q$-world. We note that according to the structural equation $S = \neg Q \wedge \neg R$, s will be true in those worlds where $\neg q$ and $\neg r$ hold. Since S's strategy is to enforce the structural equation, we know that it will hold in all accessible worlds. In addition, R's strategy continues to dictate that from every world, any accessible world will have the same valuation of R. We conclude that the sentence is true in those worlds where $R = 0$; these include the actual world w_{10x}.

Then suppose the sentence "If kangaroos had no tails but used crutches, they would not topple over" is uttered. Again, we update the strategy function for Q to add move 0. But since 0 was previously added when evaluating the first sentence, this revision has no effect. Next, we add the move 1 to all worlds in R's strategy, similarly as before. Now we evaluate the strict conditional $\Box((\neg q \wedge r) \to \neg s)$. Since S's strategy still has not changed, the causal law $S = \neg Q \wedge \neg R$ continues to hold in every accessible world. Therefore, for every world in our model, in every accessible world where $(\neg q \wedge r)$ is true, $\neg s$ is true, and so is the sentence.

What if the order of the two sentences were reversed? First, starting again from the initial conditions, the sentence "If kangaroos had no tails but used crutches, they would not topple over" is uttered. Because move 0 had not been added yet, it is this sentence that adds 0 to Q's strategy. All other effects of uttering this sentence are the same as before, as is the set of possible worlds where it is true. However, we can see a difference in the evaluation of the second sentence "If kangaroos had no tails, they would topple over". Updating the strategy function for Q has no effect, since the move 0 has already been added to Q's strategy by the first sentence. Furthermore, it is no longer the case that R's strategy keeps the valuation of R constant; as a result of the first sentence, move 1 is now available to R at every world. In other words, among the $\neg q$-worlds accessible from any given world, one of them will also be an r-world. Since $S = \neg Q \wedge \neg R$ holds in every world, we know that from any world, one of the accessible $\neg q$-worlds will not be an s-world. We conclude that the sentence does not hold in any world.

4 Discussion

4.1 Translating counterfactual sentences into str-formulas

One challenge in synthesizing a causal modeling approach to counterfactuals with a possible-worlds semantics is the difference in how counterfactual sentences are evaluated in the two approaches. Under the classic possible-worlds framework, we check whether in the closest possible worlds where the antecedent is true (making any changes to the accessibility relation, if necessary, to ensure that at least one such possible world exists), the consequent is true. In a causal theory of counterfactuals, the antecedent of the counterfactual determines the intervention to be applied to the causal model. Then, the consequent is evaluated relative to the new model.

In this paper, we identified the necessary change in the accessibility relation with the intervention in the causal model, which we implement as a change in strategy for some player. Such an approach raises two questions. The first question concerns which possible worlds count as worlds where the antecedent is true. In the kangaroo example, when we translated a counterfactual of the form $\phi > \psi$ into an **str**-formula, the strict conditional portion of the formula was simply $\Box(\phi \rightarrow \psi)$. In other words, if the antecedent of the counterfactual is ϕ, then we check whether the accessible ϕ-worlds are also ψ-worlds. However, there is evidence that this approach may not work for all scenarios.

Briggs (2012) discusses the scenario, originally found in Pearl (2000), of an execution of a prisoner. A full description of the scenario can be found in either of the above papers; we note here that there are two executioners, X and Y, and whether they fire is determined by whether the captain C signals for them to do so. In other words, the behavior of executioner X is governed by the structural equation $X = C$. If either executioner fires, the prisoner dies. In the actual world, the captain signals, both executioners fire, and the prisoner dies.

Briggs considers the sentence "If executioner X had fired, then (even) if the captain had not signalled, the prisoner would have died." Under a causal model, we intervene to change the structural equation $X = C$ to $X = 1$. However, in the classic possible-worlds framework, no change in the accessibility relation is necessary. Executioner X fires in the actual world, and as a consequence of (weak) *centering*, the assumption that every world is at least as similar to itself as to any other world, every world is then accessible to itself. Under the classic approach, we check the truth of the consequent in the closest possible world where the antecedent is true; i.e., the actual world, where the consequent is false. But as Briggs notes, applying the intervention to the causal model changes the truth of the consequent.

When specifying a set of possible worlds corresponding to a causal model, we must distinguish between worlds where different causal laws hold. For example, in the kangaroo scenario, we distinguish worlds w_{10x} (where kangaroos do not topple over because they have tails) and w_{100} (where they do not topple over, because it is a law of nature that they never topple over), even though the same propositions are true in both worlds: $L(w_{100}) = L(w_{10x}) = \{q\}$. Likewise, the antecedent of the counterfactual in the execution case is the proposition that executioner X fires; let us call it x. We note that x does not determine what structural equation holds in a particular world; in some x-worlds, the relevant causal law is $X = 1$, while in others, it is $X = C$. When we say "if executioner X had fired" in a causal model, the relevant possible worlds are those in which the structural equation is $X = 1$. The corresponding proposition is not x, but a different proposition (call it x_1), which is true in exactly those worlds where the causal law $X = 1$ holds.

4.2 Counterfactuals with complex antecedents

Second, we note that antecedents of counterfactuals are propositions (of type `Prop`), while strategies have type `World -> [Move]`. Is there a way to systematically translate propositions into strategies? We have already seen that for atomic propositions such as r, we intervene to make sure that there is an accessible world where r is true, by adding the move 1 to the strategy of player R at every world: $\lambda w.1$. Similarly, for negations of atomic propositions, such as $\neg q$, we add move 0 to Q's strategy: $\lambda w.0$.

We have also seen an example of a conjunction, $(\neg q \wedge r)$. To ensure that there is an accessible world where the conjunction holds, we simply have both players change their strategies in sequence: $(\mathbf{str}_Q(\lambda w.0))(\mathbf{str}_R(\lambda w.1))$.... We note that the order each player changes their strategy does not matter. The moves each player is allowed to make are affected only by their own strategy, not those of any other players, and the strict conditional portion of the counterfactual formula is only evaluated after all strategy changes.

For other complex antecedents, Briggs (2012) borrows the idea of a *state space* from Fine (2012). States are defined by a valuation of some variable(s); e.g., $Q = 0 \wedge R = 1$. For propositional antecedents (including negations, conjunctions, disjunctions, and material conditionals), Briggs specifies states that make the antecedent true. For example, a disjunctive antecedent $(\phi \vee \psi)$ is made true by three states or interventions: one that sets $\phi = 1$, one that sets $\psi = 1$, and one that sets both $\phi = 1 \wedge \psi = 1$.

One challenge that arises in adapting this approach to ours is that evaluating the disjunction involves checking the results of three different interventions applied to the original model. However, in our dynamic semantics, once an intervention is made, the moves added to the player's strategy remain available to future evaluations; there is no "going back" to try a different intervention. In addition, while the states associated with the disjunction $(\phi \vee \psi)$ are the same as those associated with the negated conjunction $\neg(\neg\phi \wedge \neg\psi)$, Ciardelli et al. (2018) provide evidence that those antecedents in fact have different meanings.

Furthermore, it is not clear what impact, if any, a disjunctive antecedent should have on the accessibility relation at all. Ciardelli et al. (2018) discuss the example of two switches for a light. They are connected in such a way that the light is on if the switches are both up or both down, and off otherwise. In the actual world, the switches are both up and the light is on. While Ciardelli et al. do not consider sequences of counterfactuals, it is easy enough to construct a reverse Sobel sequence as with the kangaroos:

(4) If switch A and switch B were both down, the light would be on.
#If switch A was down, the light would be off.

Now let us replace the conjunction with a disjunction. In their experiment, Ciardelli et al. found that the sentence "If switch A or switch B was down, the light would be off." was judged by most participants to be true (in contrast with the sentence "If switch A and switch B were not both up, the light would be off.", with a negated conjunctive antecedent). If we use this sentence instead in our sequence, the infelicity seems to go away:

(5) If switch A or switch B was down, the light would be off.
If switch A was down, the light would be off.

In fact, according to the rule of simplification of disjunctive antecedents, the second sentence is a logical consequence of the first. Nevertheless, this indicates that perhaps the modal horizon did not expand to include worlds where switch B was down in this case, at least not permanently; if it had, then we would have to consider them when evaluating the second sentence. Alternatively, von Fintel (2001) suggests that logical arguments, unlike normal discourse, carry with them an assumption of constant context. Certainly more research is needed in this area.

5 Conclusion

In this paper, we present a semantics for counterfactuals that combines ideas from dynamic semantics and causal modeling approaches. Our implementation is based on concurrent game structures, where variables are interpreted as players and interventions as changes in players' strategies. Using the classic example of kangaroos with no tails, we show how our approach is able to capture judgments about sequences of counterfactuals.

Acknowledgements

We would like to thank the reviewers for their helpful comments.

References

Alur, R., T. A. Henzinger, and O. Kupferman (2002, September). Alternating-time temporal logic. *Journal of the ACM 49*(5), 672–713.

Briggs, R. (2012). Interventionist counterfactuals. *Philosophical Studies 160*(1), 139–166.

Ciardelli, I., L. Zhang, and L. Champollion (2018, Dec). Two switches in the theory of counterfactuals. *Linguistics and Philosophy 41*(6), 577–621.

Fine, K. (2012). Counterfactuals without possible worlds. *The Journal of Philosophy 109*(3), 221–246.

Groenendijk, J. and M. Stokhof (1991). Dynamic predicate logic. *Linguistics and Philosophy 14*(1), 39–100.

Jamroga, W., W. van der Hoek, and M. Wooldridge (2005). Intentions and strategies in game-like scenarios. In *Portuguese Conference on Artificial Intelligence*, pp. 512–523. Springer.

Kratzer, A. (1981). Partition and revision: The semantics of counterfactuals. *Journal of Philosophical Logic 10*(2), 201–216.

Kripke, S. A. (1963). Semantical considerations on modal logic. *Acta Philosophica Fennica 16*(1963), 83–94.

Lewis, D. (1973). *Counterfactuals.* Blackwell.

Pearl, J. (2000). *Causality.* Cambridge University Press.

Pearl, J. and D. Mackenzie (2018). *The Book of Why: The New Science of Cause and Effect.* Basic Books.

Pollock, J. (1976). *Subjunctive reasoning.* Springer.

Stalnaker, R. C. (1968). A theory of conditionals. In W. L. Harper, R. Stalnaker, and G. Pearce (Eds.), *Ifs: Conditionals, Belief, Decision, Chance and Time*, pp. 41–55. Dordrecht: Springer Netherlands.

von Fintel, K. (2001). Counterfactuals in a dynamic context. *Current Studies in Linguistics Series 36*, 123–152.

Visual TTR
Modelling Visual Question Answering in Type Theory with Records

Ronja Utescher
Bielefeld University
r.utescher@uni-bielefeld.de

April 1, 2019

Abstract

In this paper, I will describe a system that was developed for the task of Visual Question Answering. The system uses the rich type universe of Type Theory with Records (TTR) to model utterances about the image, the image itself, and classifications made relating the outcomes of these two tasks. At its most basic, the decision of whether any given predicate can be assigned to an object in the image is delegated to a CNN. Consequently, images can be taken as evidence for propositional judgments. The end result is a model whose application of perceptual classifiers to a given image is guided by the accompanying utterance.

1 Introduction

Visual question answering is a recent popular task in the field of computer vision. However, the extent to which formal linguistics is needed to solve the task has been a point of contention. This paper details an approach that utilizes both a rule-based approach to parsing utterances about an image and a deep neural model to supply perceptual meaning. TTR (Cooper and Ginzburg, 2015) offers a powerful semantic framework for modelling natural language. TTR has been used to model more coarse-grained linguistic phenomena, many of them related to dialogue. However, this paper is concerned with relatively basic phenomena. The challenge here is to model a multimodal world, namely a visual and linguistic one.

This project builds on a previous VQA model using TTR which is detailed in Matsson (2018)[1]. Both projects utilize pyTTR (Cooper, 2017), a python implementation of TTR. This previous implementation features a pipeline that includes object recognition in the form of You Only Look Once (YOLO, Redmon et al. (2015)), representation of the image and question in TTR and, subsequently, evaluation of the utterance with respect to the image. The TTR representation of the image consists of a record type that contains an individual variable and bounding box for every detected object, as well as the predicates that apply to them. Furthermore, it uses the predicate *loc* to link individual variables to their bounding boxes. This predicate simply signifies that the individual with this name is *located* at this position in the image. I refine the TTR modelling of the image and object classification and replace YOLO with a set of binary word classifiers. In Visual TTR, predicates do not need to be added explicitly to the TTR representation of the image. Instead, links between the image and the question are made where appropriate. For example, if a question contains a reference to a dog, the system will try to find suitable objects by running the dog classifier on every annotated entity in the image. If the classifier returns a sufficiently high score for any of the objects, these objects are considered instances of the *dog* predicate (type). These technical changes enable a change to the order in which the model performs its sub-tasks. Where the original system runs an object recognition algorithm on the image and translates the result to a TTR representation of the image, the question is now parsed first, and guides the perceptual classification part of the architecture.

[1]see `https://github.com/arildm/imagettr`

In section 3, I make recommendations for appropriate training data and classifier design. Based on the classifier score, likely candidate regions will be considered instances (or witnesses) of the predicate type. In the case of polar questions, this classified record of the image is a witness of the question type iff the answer to the question is *yes*.

Matsson (2018)	Visual TTR
object recognition	bounding box annotations
$\downarrow$ *bounding boxes, predicates, entities*	$\downarrow$ *bounding boxes, entities*
image type	image record
question parsing	question parsing
-	object classification
type check	type check
$\downarrow$ *answer*	$\downarrow$ *answer*

Figure 1: Comparison of ImageTTR and Visual TTR Pipelines

2 A Visual Universe of Types

In order to implement the visual classification in TTR, all information necessary for classification should be contained in the representation of the image. While it would be possible to include the entire image matrix, this model uses the path to the image for legibility reasons. This section provides an overview of the types (and types of types) that are used in the model. Basic Types are basic in the sense that they do not depend on other types and should be thought of as corresponding to basic ontological categories (Cooper and Ginzburg, 2015).

2.1 Basic Types

Image(path) The source of the image data.

Int Integers, used to describe the coordinates of the bounding boxes.

Ind Variables of type *Ind* are Montagovian individuals. In the record for a given image, every object is assigned an identifier or name. In the case of the examples in this paper, this name uses the object ids annotated in the corpus (see section 3.1).

2.2 The Image in TTR

2.2.1 Segment & Region

The model utilizes segmented images, as are commonly provided with state-of-the-art image corpora like MS COCO (Lin et al., 2014) or Visual Genome (Krishna et al., 2016).

The segment contains the (x,y) coordinates of the bottom-left corner as well as the width and height of the bounding box, as well as the path to the image. Note that this constitutes all the visual information about the relevant part of the image.

The region contains a segment and its name, a variable of type *Ind*. The two fields in the *Region* type represent the segment *seg* and the name *z* of the object in question.

$$\left[\begin{array}{lll} seg & : & \left[\begin{array}{rcl} x & : & Int \\ y & : & Int \\ w & : & Int \\ h & : & Int \\ path & : & Image \end{array}\right] \\ z & : & Ind \end{array}\right] \tag{1}$$

2.2.2 Scene

The Scene type consists of at least one *Ind* type and a corresponding *Region* type object. The Scene is the TTR representation of the entire image and contains the information of every object in the image. Note that the names of each object appear twice in this format. This has two purposes. One, the image itself also contains the individuals; two, the individual is now clearly linked to its segment.
When processing an image, a record/an instance of the *Scene* type is produced. In an image with only two objects, this could look like (2).

$$\begin{bmatrix} obj_0 & = & \begin{bmatrix} seg & = & \begin{bmatrix} x & = & 349 \\ y & = & 138 \\ w & = & 71 \\ h & = & 90 \\ path & = & image.jpg \end{bmatrix} \\ z & = & a_{1032844} \end{bmatrix} \\ obj_1 & = & \begin{bmatrix} seg & = & \begin{bmatrix} x & = & 3 \\ y & = & 146 \\ w & = & 204 \\ h & = & 90 \\ path & = & image.jpg \end{bmatrix} \\ z & = & a_{1032847} \end{bmatrix} \\ z_0 & = & a_{1032844} \\ z_1 & = & a_{1032847} \end{bmatrix} \tag{2}$$

3 Visual Grounding

3.1 Training Data

Visual Genome (Krishna et al., 2016) is a densely annotated dataset of 108k images. The dataset contains several kinds of human-generated annotations such as region descriptions and question/answer pairs. However, the model described in this paper works solely with object annotations. The object annotations consist of a name and bounding box. The object names are extracted from region descriptions by crowd-workers. The format I used for preprocessing these annotations can be found in the repository released alongside Schlangen (2019).[2]

3.2 Object Classification

In contrast to Matsson (2018), the model described in this paper uses object classifiers. Conceptually, these represent the system's understanding of the perceptual meaning of object names. This means that a separate classifier must be trained for every word in the system's vocabulary. This particular implementation uses word classifiers with a architecture much like that described in (Schlangen et al., 2016)[3]. These classifiers are binary logistic regression classifiers based on vgg19 (Simonyan and Zisserman, 2014) features. The classifiers share a common base model that outputs the visual features, while the final layer is different for every word(-model).
Opting for these classifiers over the YOLO-model leads to more control over the vocabulary. YOLO uses the PASCAL VOC (Everingham et al., 2015) test set of twenty object categories. The perceptual classifiers also do not have a structural bias against infrequent categories in the training data.

[2] However, I trained classifiers on a subset of the roughly 3.8 million object annotations.

[3] Although the architectures are similar, the data and application of the models turn out quite differently. Compared to reference resolution task that the word classifiers from Schlangen et al. (2016) were used for, object naming is a comparatively simpler task.

4 Classification in Visual TTR

4.1 Perceptual Segments

For every predicate, there is a corresponding Basic Type that maps from visual data (in this case, a *seg* record) to a basic perceptual type. It is here that pyTTR invokes the classifier. For example, the conditions for being a *DogSeg* are (1) be a *seg*, (2) get a higher-than-threshold score from the dog classifier (see (3)). This is not yet applicable to the question - it represents the perceptually basic type of *looking like a dog*.

$$\begin{bmatrix} seg & : & \begin{bmatrix} x & : & Int \\ y & : & Int \\ w & : & Int \\ h & : & Int \\ path & : & Image \end{bmatrix} \end{bmatrix} : DogSeg\ if\ clsfr(seg) > threshold \tag{3}$$

4.2 Predicates

Classification, one of the major cornerstones of the model, has the power to add regions to the witness cache of a given predicate. In order to add entities to the witness cache, potential candidate regions are queried. If the result of the query is positive, the region's record is considered a witness of the predicate (see (4)).

$$\begin{bmatrix} seg & = & \begin{bmatrix} x & = & 10 \\ y & = & 9 \\ w & = & 473 \\ h & = & 300 \\ path & = & image.jpg \end{bmatrix} \\ z & = & a_{1032844} \end{bmatrix} : \begin{bmatrix} c & : & dog(z) \end{bmatrix} \tag{4}$$

4.3 Objects as Witnesses of a PType

In the previous section, I show how regions of the image can be identified as evidence for a certain predicate. However, this alone does not cover any TTR parse of a question. To illustrate, think of a basic example - *Is there a dog?*. This should be modelled like so:

$$\begin{bmatrix} z & : & Ind \\ c & : & \langle \lambda v : Ind.dog(v), z \rangle \end{bmatrix} \tag{5}$$

If the system has already classified one of the *obj*s as being of type *c : dog(z)* and there exists a corresponding *z* in the image record, the system will come to the conclusion that the image is in fact a witness for the question type:

$$\begin{bmatrix} obj_2 & = & \begin{bmatrix} seg & = & \begin{bmatrix} x & = & 10 \\ y & = & 9 \\ w & = & 473 \\ h & = & 300 \\ path & = & image.jpg \end{bmatrix} \\ z & = & a_{1032844} \end{bmatrix} \\ z_2 & = & a_{1032844} \end{bmatrix} : \begin{bmatrix} z & : & Ind \\ c & : & \langle \lambda v : Ind.dog(v), z \rangle \end{bmatrix} \tag{6}$$

As shown in (6), classification in Visual TTR is a type judgment. Iff the answer to the question is *yes*, the image is a Record of the Record Type of the question. For example, the picture is an instance of the *kind of situations where there is a dog*. The surface representation of the image does not change. However, type judgments were made - on the basis of the question, the perceptual classifiers and the image. Figure 2 (above) provides a visualization of the information that the model uses to make a determination about the predicate type. The image, the object bounding boxes, and the scores produced by the classifier.

Figure 2: (Above) The image, with bounding boxes and the scores of the *dog*-classifier.

(Right) The formal representation of the image, with bounding boxes (*x*,*y*,*w*,*h*), the *path*, and the object ids (z).

$$\left[\begin{array}{lcl} obj_0 & = & \left[\begin{array}{lcl} seg & = & \left[\begin{array}{lcl} x & = & 252 \\ y & = & 47 \\ w & = & 142 \\ h & = & 260 \\ path & = & 2401247.jpg \end{array}\right] \\ z & = & a_{401400} \end{array}\right] \\ z_0 & = & a_{401400} \\ obj_1 & = & \left[\begin{array}{lcl} seg & = & \left[\begin{array}{lcl} x & = & 116 \\ y & = & 143 \\ w & = & 130 \\ h & = & 166 \\ path & = & 2401247.jpg \end{array}\right] \\ z & = & a_{401401} \end{array}\right] \\ z_1 & = & a_{401401} \\ obj_2 & = & \left[\begin{array}{lcl} seg & = & \left[\begin{array}{lcl} x & = & 10 \\ y & = & 9 \\ w & = & 473 \\ h & = & 300 \\ path & = & 2401247.jpg \end{array}\right] \\ z & = & a_{401403} \end{array}\right] \\ z_2 & = & a_{401403} \\ obj_3 & = & \left[\begin{array}{lcl} seg & = & \left[\begin{array}{lcl} x & = & 415 \\ y & = & 7 \\ w & = & 76 \\ h & = & 44 \\ path & = & 2401247.jpg \end{array}\right] \\ z & = & a_{401416} \end{array}\right] \\ z_3 & = & a_{401416} \end{array}\right]$$

5 Conclusions

While the system described in this paper is not yet a full-fledged Q&A system, it shows that TTR is a suitable formalism for the task of building and querying an understanding of an image. In order to reliably measure the effectiveness of the model, a proper training set is necessary. For example, this could mean the significant expansion of its grammar so that is covers a Visual Q&A dataset such as VQA v2 (Goyal et al., 2017). The expansion of the grammar is desirable also because being able to model more semantic nuance (e.g. background/foreground) is one of the major benefits of using TTR in the first place.

In this paper, I pay particular attention to the formal core of this system. A necessary aspect of such a model that I have glossed over is the parser. There is no off-the-shelf English to TTR parser, so the model does require the person implementing it to write a grammar. This has the disadvantage of limiting the model's coverage (and having to write a grammar). The advantage of a custom grammar is that it is possible to model domain-specific semantic phenomena. For example, *Is there a cat?* and *Is this a cat?* evoke the same classifier. The former applies the classifier to the whole image, while the latter applies it to all objects in the image.

A further upside to the model proposed here is transparency. It is possible for a human observer to examine the judgments that the model made when trying to answer a question. This is not very exciting in the *dog* example, but should become useful for questions that require multiple perceptual type judgments. Another avenue for further work on the model would be to implement it in an agent-based system as described in Matsson (2018). In such a setting, judgments made about an image can become persistent additions to the agent's knowledge base.

References

Cooper, R. (2017). PyTTR. https://github.com/GU-CLASP/pyttr.

Cooper, R. and J. Ginzburg (2015). *Type Theory with Records for Natural Language Semantics**, Chapter 12, pp. 375–407. John Wiley & Sons, Ltd.

Everingham, M., S. M. A. Eslami, L. Van Gool, C. K. I. Williams, J. Winn, and A. Zisserman (2015). The pascal visual object classes challenge: A retrospective. *International Journal of Computer Vision 111*(1), 98–136.

Goyal, Y., T. Khot, D. Summers-Stay, D. Batra, and D. Parikh (2017). Making the V in VQA matter: Elevating the role of image understanding in Visual Question Answering. In *Conference on Computer Vision and Pattern Recognition (CVPR)*.

Krishna, R., Y. Zhu, O. Groth, J. Johnson, K. Hata, J. Kravitz, S. Chen, Y. Kalantidis, L.-J. Li, D. A. Shamma, M. Bernstein, and L. Fei-Fei (2016). Visual genome: Connecting language and vision using crowdsourced dense image annotations.

Lin, T., M. Maire, S. J. Belongie, L. D. Bourdev, R. B. Girshick, J. Hays, P. Perona, D. Ramanan, P. Dollár, and C. L. Zitnick (2014). Microsoft COCO: common objects in context. *CoRR abs/1405.0312*.

Matsson, A. (2018). Implementing perceptual semantics in type theory with records). Master's thesis, University of Gothenburg.

Redmon, J., S. K. Divvala, R. B. Girshick, and A. Farhadi (2015). You only look once: Unified, real-time object detection. *CoRR abs/1506.02640*.

Schlangen, D. (2019). Natural language semantics with pictures: Some language vision datasets and potential uses for computational semantics.

Schlangen, D., S. Zarriess, and C. Kennington (2016). Resolving references to objects in photographs using the words-as-classifiers model.

Simonyan, K. and A. Zisserman (2014). Very deep convolutional networks for large-scale image recognition.

The Lexical Gap: An Improved Measure of Automated Image Description Quality

Austin Kershaw
University of Surrey
ak00789@surrey.ac.uk

Miroslaw Bober
University of Surrey
mbober@surrey.ac.uk

April 1, 2019

Abstract

The challenge of automatically describing images and videos has stimulated much research in Computer Vision and Natural Language Processing. In order to test the semantic abilities of new algorithms, we need reliable and objective ways of measuring progress. Using our dataset of 2K human and machine descriptions, we find that standard evaluation measures alone do not adequately measure the semantic richness of a description. We introduce and test a new measure of semantic ability based on relative lexical diversity. We show how our measure can work alongside existing measures to achieve state of the art correlation with human judgement of quality.

1 Introduction

Image and video processing systems are being developed for a wide variety of semantically rich tasks, such storytelling (Zhu et al., 2015), Visual Question Answering (VQA) (Anderson et al., 2017; Teney et al., 2016; Wu et al., 2016), and engaging in visual dialogue (Jain et al., 2018). In this paper, we consider the task of Image Description (Lin et al., 2014; Hodosh et al., 2015; Plummer et al., 2017). Closing the semantic gap between human and machine descriptions requires robust and standardised measures of performance. In classical computer vision problems such as object detection, segmentation and classification, quality can be defined easily as a comparison between machine predictions and reference answers. Standard measures of image description quality consider the alignment of candidate sentences with ground truth sentences. However defining a set of "correct" answers for a given image is restrictive, as an image may contain diverse semantic information. Consequently we find semantically rich and detailed content is regarded very poorly by such measures, and the more sparse and simplistic the reference data and predictions, the higher the score. In summary:

1. We sourced 2K human and machine descriptions, which we used to show that standard automated measures of quality give an incomplete picture of semantic ability. The measures produce higher scores when candidates and reference data are semantically sparse, and lower scores on richer descriptions.
2. We show that measuring the relative lexical diversity of a system is a better indicator of semantic ability. We define two measures of relative diversity, and show that when combined with standard measures, achieve achieve state-of-the-art correlation with human judgement.

We hope our work will stimulate research in to more advanced measures of semantic ability, helping to close the gap between human and machine descriptions.

2 Relevant Literature

The predominant approach to generating original descriptions is to encode visual data into semantically useful features, which are then decoded into language. The capability of Convolutional Neural

Networks (CNN) and their variants for extracting spatial features is well established in Computer Vision. Pre-training the network on a dataset such as ImageNet[1] (which already embeds images based on the WordNet nouns contained within them) provides spatial features which accurately predict common nouns. In language generation, it is common to use a gated recurrent neural network which predicts a probability distribution across the vocabulary, given prior states and spatial features (Long et al., 2014). Many systems have evolved from this fundamental approach, and we refer interested readers to surveys on such developments(Bernardi et al., 2016; Aafaq et al., 2018). Systems are typically trained end-to-end on one of a number of image description datasets. Relevant to this paper are MS-COCO (Lin et al., 2014), Flickr8k (Hodosh et al., 2015), and Flickr30k(Plummer et al., 2017).

2.1 Methods of Evaluation

Objective measures of performance enable the automatic evaluation of systems across large datasets, avoiding the laborious process of sourcing human judgements. The measures divide into three groups:

1. Machine Translation measures: Early description systems considered image description as a translation task, in which information in the visual domain, is translated to the linguistic domain. As such machine translation measures based on n-gram alignment such as BLEU(Papineni et al., 2002), ROUGE(Lin and Hovy, 2003) and METEOR(Denkowski and Lavie, 2014).

2. Captioning Measures: CIDEr(Vedantam et al., 2015) and SPICE(Anderson et al., 2016), designed specifically for the description task. CIDEr addresses the problem of description diversity by rewarding candidates that match the consensus of references. SPICE, applies work from scene graph generation(Schuster et al., 2015) to create semantic graph representations of candidate and ground truth.

3. Neural Network Evaluation: Neural networks can be trained to evaluate descriptions. NNEVAL (Sharif et al., 2018) is a network trained to predict whether a description is human or machine, using both the captioning and translation measures as linguistic features.

As automated measures are a substitute for human evaluation, they are compared on the basis of their ability to correlate with human judgement. The poor correlation of translation measures is well known, (Bernardi et al., 2016; Chen and Dolan, 2011), and captioning measures show improved results. In this work we assess the correlation using the Composite dataset(Aditya et al., 2015). Human and machine captions for images in subsets of MS-COCO, Flickr8K and Flickr30K are judged by Amazon Mechanical Turk workers, and rated for correctness and completeness.

2.2 Lexical Diversity (LD)

The ability of text or speech to convey information specifically and articulately is a widely studied field. It is of interest in areas such as language learning, educational psychology and the study of speech impediments (Durán et al., 2004; Jarvis, 2013). An indicator of such fluency is Lexical Diversity (LD), which is a measure of the distribution of words used in a sample text. A simple measure such as the Type Token Ratio (TTR) considers the number of unique words used, relative to the total number of words in a sample. However TTR disadvantages longer texts, because for every additional word added to a corpus, the probability that it will be novel decreases. Such a measure would therefore be difficult to apply to a large scale image description corpus. A variety of measures derived from TTR have been proposed to address the issue of sample size such as the rate at which the TTR falls as successive tokens are added to the text (Jarvis, 2013). A curve with a larger negative gradient demonstrates more diversity than one with a smaller decay, and its parameters can be found with a numerical method (Durán et al., 2004). We later illustrate the application of this to image descriptions. More recent measures such as MTLD (McCarthy and Jarvis, 2010) consider the mean length of word strings for a particular TTR.

[1]http://www.image-net.org/

Hypo-geometric Distribution-D (HD-D) (McCarthy and Jarvis, 2010) measures the probability that for a random sample of words from a corpus, a particular token will be selected a certain number of times. Here we use HD-D for its simple implementation, lower sensitivity to corpus size and wide use in the literature, but our method could be applied with a different LD measure.

3 Evaluation Measures and Rich Descriptions

A desirable quality of a description is to convey semantically insightful information. In this section we describe how we sourced a set of human and machine descriptions, comparing them on their semantic richness. We compared standard evaluation measures on semantically sparse and rich captions.

3.1 Sourcing Rich and Sparse Descriptions

We showed a total of 20 images to volunteers (Figure 1), asking them to describe the image in an informative sentence. "*Describe this image as if describing it to a friend*". Unlike large scale data collection, where participants have many images to process, our smaller scale collection gave participants unlimited time to consider their description. We also sourced machine descriptions by training a common image captioning baseline(Xu et al., 2016) on MS-COCO. After validating the performance of our system against the original paper, we sourced 1K machine descriptions of our images. From a subjective comparison between the human and machine descriptions, we noted a gap in semantic richness, illustrated in Figure 2. Humans incorporate information extrinsic to the images, such as from current affairs, cultural background and human experience, reacting with empathy to emotional cues. Machine descriptions however, are produced sequentially one word at a time, with each word selected from a probability distribution, predicted from object and attribute features. As all human descriptions were semantically more insightful than corresponding machine descriptions, we refer the machine descriptions as "sparse" and human descriptions as "rich". Table 2 shows that the distinction between rich and sparse is also evident in the vocabulary and lexical diversity of the datasets.

Figure 1: Rich-Sparse Dataset

3.2 Evaluation Measures on Human and Machine Descriptions

We evaluated human and machine descriptions separately, using the standard evaluation measures. For each image we performed 1000 evaluations, where 5 sentences were randomly selected from the set of descriptions to be the ground truth candidates, with the remaining used to calculate the metrics. Table 1 shows that when both ground truth and candidate description sentences are semantically sparse they perform very well. However descriptions of a higher semantic complexity are penalised as a result of their more diverse and rich descriptions, with many insightful descriptions scoring zero. Figure 3 shows examples where the SPICE metric scores rich descriptions as zero. When rich descriptions were used as ground truth, the machine descriptions perform very poorly.

3.3 Comparison of Lexical Diversity

We measured and compared the LD of human and machine descriptions. Our human descriptions were universally richer and more semantically detailed than the machine descriptions. For each of the 40 TTR

This is a picture of three young men carrying a coffin
The faces of two of the boys who can be seen look serious
Some boys or young men are in a funeral procession

A man is in a hat and hat and tie
A man is talking on a cell phone
Man wearing sunglasses and a red hat with a hat on
A men wearing a red hat and sunglasses

A married couple are celebrating an anniversary
The wome is posing as if she is going to cut the cake
A man and a women are standing next to each other in front of a white cake

Three men are standing around a table with a cake on it
A man cutting a cake on a white table
Three men are standing around a table with a cake on it

A group of Asian Students are preparing to do a class test
They are each reading from a paper which may be a test or an exam
A group exercise which requires students to talk to each other
A group of girls are busy with their classroom activity

A group of kids sitting on a table with laptops
A group of people are sitting around a table
Several people are sitting around a table eating a meal

A young woman is sitting on the floor with a her back against a table leg
A woman is looking sorrowful
The floor is woodern and there are some wooden tables and chairs in the room

The woman is holding a baby and a young boy sitting on the floor
A woman sitting on a wooden bench next to a woman
A little girl sitting on a wooden bench

Figure 2: Examples of human (black) and machine descriptions (red).

A political march is taking place
A protest is taking place
A man is speaking to the marchers through a police traffic cone
A protest scene on a tree lined city street
One protester is using a traffic cone as a megaphone
One woman is holding two flip-flops up in the air
People are shouting and chanting
People are waving their hands in the air and shouting
A man shouting has is holding his arms out and shouting

A crowd of people are standing around a large crowd.
A group of people on a city street.
A group of people on the street with umbrellas
A group of people standing next to a crowd of people.
Many people are walking on a sidewalk with a crowd of people watching.

Figure 3: Zero scoring rich descriptions (top) and low scoring machine descriptions (bottom) when measured on SPICE

curves we plotted (machine and human for each image), we found that LD was an accurate indication of whether a descriptions was from the rich or sparse set. Figure 4 shows the TTR curves for the examples presented in Figure 2 . The figure illustrates the faster decline of the sparse descriptions, relative to the semantically richer descriptions.

Ground Truth	Human		Machine	
Candidates	Human	Machine	Human	Machine
Cider	0.09	0.02	0.01	0.27
Bleu1	0.49	0.37	0.25	0.75
Bleu2	0.22	0.1	0.06	0.59
Bleu3	0.09	0.01	0.01	0.42
Bleu4	0.05	0.00	0.00	0.28
Rouge(L)	0.32	0.23	0.19	0.19
METEOR	0.17	0.1	0.09	0.3
SPICE	0.1	0.05	0.03	0.2

Table 1: Evaluation Measures for Rich (Human) and Sparse(Machine) Domains

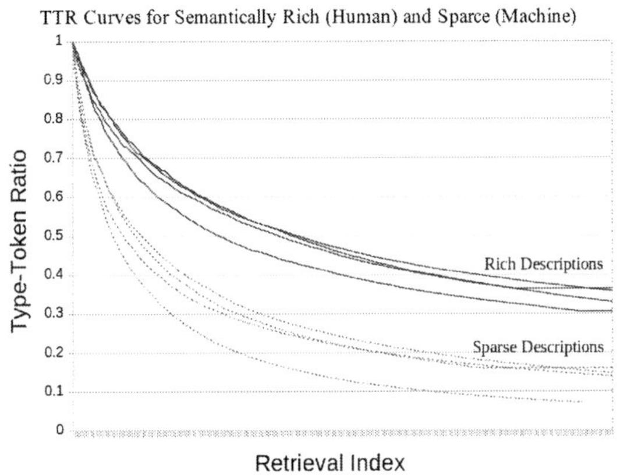

Figure 4: TTR curves for rich and sparse descriptions

3.4 Comparison of Linguistic Complexity

Readability measures have long been used to automatically grade the complexity of language. We tested several measures, including Flesch–Kincaid(Kincaid JP, 1988), Coleman–Liau(Coleman and Liau, 1975), Dale-Chall(Dale E, 1948) and Automated Readability(Senter, 1967). However we found they did not correlate well with semantic quality. Informative descriptions tend to be lexically diverse, but are not necessarily complex. Rich descriptions can contain a higher syllable count and more 'difficult' words than sparse descriptions however this is not always the case. Furthermore a description corpus which generates exactly the same complex sentence for every image conveys no information and yet would score highly on complexity.

4 The Lexical Gap

One indication of the performance of a machine description system, is its ability to convey semantically rich information. We propose a measure which considers the entire output of a description system (which

	Lexical Diversity				
	TTR	Root-TTR	Log-TTR	HDD	MTLD
Sparse	0.09	2.98	0.65	0.55	16.07
Rich	0.24	14.29	0.83	0.75	40.58

Table 2: Rich-Sparse Dataset Statistics

we call c_m) and compares it with its training data (which we call c_r). Thus instead of solely considering a machine's ability to predict n-grams or words, we also measure its ability to maintain the linguistic diversity of its training corpus. Our key finding is that measuring the LD of a description corpus relative to its ground truth data is a good indication of semantic quality, and can be used to weight standard performance measures, increasing their correlation with human subjective judgement. In this section we define our measures, which we later compare compare with standard captioning measures.

4.1 Measuring the Lexical Gap

The Lexical Diversity Ratio (LDR) is a straightforward measure of the ability of a machine to match the semantic depth of its source material. Given a function L which calculates LD for a reference description corpus c_r and the machine description corpus c_m, we define the Lexical Diversity Ratio (LDR) l_d as:

$$l_d = \frac{L(c_m)}{L(c_r)} \tag{1}$$

A machine with a score of 1, is more able to match the lexical diversity of its training source. A lower score, indicates a reduction in semantic richness. We also define the lexical gap (L_g) a bounded measure of the ability of a system to maintain lexical diversity. An l_d below some constant μ, will tend to zero indicating a larger lexical gap. As l_d increases a system is closing that gap, towards a score of 1, which indicates ideal performance. Given the constants μ and α, we define the Lexical Gap L_g:

$$L_g = \frac{1}{1 + \exp^{-\alpha(l_d - \mu)}} \tag{2}$$

Considering our rich and sparse descriptions independently, we split them into sub-corpora. We calculate l_d scores each sub-corpora as (c_r) using in every case the richer descriptions has our reference c_r. Figure 5 shows the LDRs (l_d) for the rich and sparse parts of our description dataset. The richer descriptions, although more broadly distributed, have a higher mean l_d. We define μ as the value that produces the Bayes Minimum error between the two distributions of l_d (0.81), and we set α=5 to distribute all our values broadly and between the range 0..1. Then given a description metric M, we calculate the gap-

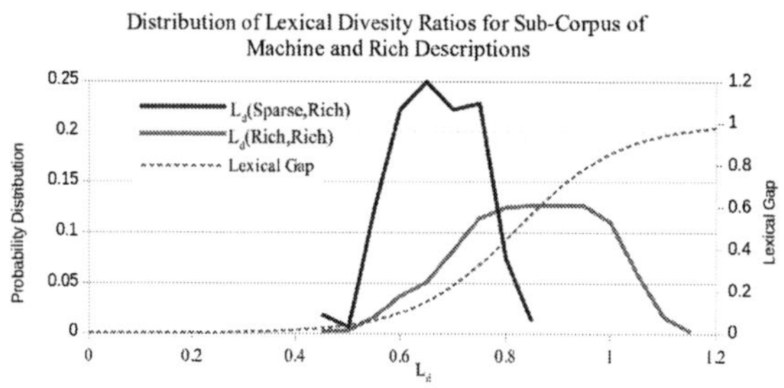

Figure 5: Distribution of LDR scores for sparse and rich descriptions

weighted score for each sentence: s_n in a corpus $s_n \subseteq c_r$:

$$m_{gap} = M(s_n)L_g \tag{3}$$

$$m_{ldr} = M(s_n)L_d \tag{4}$$

5 Results

We evaluated the performance of weighted lexical measures using the Composite dataset. The dataset contains selected human and machine descriptions for images sourced from Flickr30k, Flickr8K and

Source Dataset	Caption Source	LDR (l_d)	Lexical Gap (L_g)
Flickr30k	Human	1.03	0.98
	Machine1	0.63	0.02
	Machine2	0.70	0.08
	Machine3	0.71	0.11
Flickr8k	Human	0.92	0.89
	Machine1	0.71	0.10
	Machine2	0.65	0.03
MS COCO	Human	0.97	0.95
	Machine1	0.72	0.11
	Machine2	0.73	0.13
	Machine3	0.73	0.13

Table 3: Calculation of l_d and L_g for the Composite Dataset

	Spearman	Pearson	Kendal-T
NNEval	**0.524**	0.532	**0.404**
l_d	0.473	0.621	0.329
L_g	0.473	**0.630**	0.369

Table 4: Overall Correlations for LDR and Lexical Gap

MS COCO. For each description in Composite, we sourced the relevant ground truth sentences from the source dataset so that we could calculate the captioning scores for that sentence. These are the standard scores presented in Table 5.

Using our measures defined previously, we also calculated l_d and L_g for each subset of the Composite dataset (Table 3) using the relevant source corpus as our reference (c_r). We thus measured the lexical diversity of human and machine subsets of the Composite dataset. Before using standard evaluation measures, we found that our l_d and L_g correlated well with human subjective judgements, as presented in Table 4. Then we calculated the m_{gap} and m_{ldr} for each evaluation measure over the entire Composite dataset. We calculate the correlation performance with the human evaluation scores.

Table 5 compares the gap weighted scores with standard measures of performance. We found that on all measures, weighting by l_d and L_g improves the correlation between human judgements and objective measures.

	Spearman			Pearson			Kendal-T		
	Standard	m_{ldr}	m_{gap}	Standard	m_{ldr}	m_{gap}	Standard	m_{ldr}	m_{gap}
CIDEr	0.361	0.383	**0.516**	0.354	0.388	**0.571**	0.270	0.369	**0.389**
Bleu1	0.346	0.429	**0.444**	0.362	0.471	**0.489**	0.257	0.292	**0.362**
Bleu2	0.323	**0.395**	0.393	0.342	0.411	**0.534**	0.258	**0.283**	0.282
Bleu3	0.292	0.382	**0.516**	0.286	0.327	**0.544**	0.250	0.277	**0.392**
Bleu4	0.235	0.373	**0.531**	0.202	0.228	**0.569**	0.206	0.286	**0.401**
Rouge_L	0.364	0.447	**0.473**	0.369	0.476	**0.632**	0.271	0.319	**0.369**
Meteor	0.367	0.427	**0.473**	0.400	0.478	**0.635**	0.275	0.335	**0.369**
SPICE	0.372	0.409	**0.540**	0.399	0.448	**0.573**	0.299	0.329	**0.411**

Table 5: Overall Correlations for LDR and Lexical Gap. All p-values<0.001

6 Conclusion

Much progress has been in visual description, with many systems capable of generating original sentences which convey salient objects and attributes. However building systems capable of conveying semantically insightful information still remains a big challenge because of the difficulty of developing effective and insightful evaluation measures. We find that LD of descriptions is a useful indicator of semantic quality, and propose that description systems are measured not only on the accuracy of their predictions, but also on their ability convey lexically specific information. Measuring LD, rewards systems which are able to preserve rich and diverse descriptions, but penalises sparse systems, which have a poor lexical capability.

We hope that our work will inspire larger datasets of semantically richer and more detailed descriptions, and the development of more effective evaluation criteria for descriptions.

References

Aafaq, N., S. Z. Gilani, W. Liu, and A. Mian (2018). Video Description: A Survey of Methods, Datasets and Evaluation Metrics. pp. 1–25.

Aditya, S., Y. Ang, C. Baral, C. Fermuller, and Y. Aloimonos (2015). From Images to Sentences through Scene Description Graphs using Reasoning and Knowledge. *Arxiv*.

Anderson, P., B. Fernando, M. Johnson, and S. Gould (2016). SPICE: Semantic propositional image caption evaluation. In *Lecture Notes in Computer Science (including subseries Lecture Notes in Artificial Intelligence and Lecture Notes in Bioinformatics)*, Volume 9909 LNCS, pp. 382–398.

Anderson, P., X. He, C. Buehler, D. Teney, M. Johnson, S. Gould, and L. Zhang (2017). Bottom-Up and Top-Down Attention for Image Captioning and Visual Question Answering.

Bernardi, R., R. Cakici, D. Elliott, A. Erdem, E. Erdem, N. Ikizler-Cinbis, F. Keller, A. Muscat, and B. Plank (2016). Automatic description generation from images: A survey of models, datasets, and evaluation measures. *Journal of Artificial Intelligence Research 55*, 409–442.

Chen, D. L. and W. B. Dolan (2011). Collecting Highly Parallel Data for Paraphrase Evaluation. *Proceedings of the 49th Annual Meeting of the Association for Computational Linguistics*.

Coleman, M. and T. L. Liau (1975). A computer readability formula designed for machine scoring. *Journal of Applied Psychology Vol. 60*, pp. 283–284.

Dale E, C. J. (1948). A Formula for Predicting Readability. *Educational Research Bulletin 27*(2), 37–54.

Denkowski, M. and A. Lavie (2014). Meteor Universal: Language Specific Translation Evaluation for Any Target Language. In *WMT*, pp. 376–380.

Durán, P., D. Malvern, B. Richards, and N. Chipere (2004). Developmental trends in lexical diversity.

Hodosh, M., P. Young, and J. Hockenmaier (2015). Framing image description as a ranking task: Data, models and evaluation metrics. In *IJCAI International Joint Conference on Artificial Intelligence*, Volume 2015-Janua, pp. 4188–4192.

Jain, U., S. Lazebnik, and A. Schwing (2018). Two can play this Game: Visual Dialog with Discriminative Question Generation and Answering. In *The IEEE Conference on Computer Vision and Pattern Recognition (CVPR)*, pp. 5754–5763.

Jarvis, S. (2013). Capturing the Diversity in Lexical Diversity. *Language Learning : A journal of Research in Language 63*(1), 87–106.

Kincaid JP, Braby R, M. J. (1988). Electronic authoring and delivery of technical information. *Journal of Instructional Development*.

Lin, C.-Y. and E. Hovy (2003). Automatic evaluation of summaries using N-gram co-occurrence statistics. *Proceedings of the 2003 Conference of the North American Chapter of the Association for Computational Linguistics on Human Language Technology - NAACL '03 2003*(June), 71–78.

Lin, T. Y., M. Maire, S. Belongie, J. Hays, P. Perona, D. Ramanan, P. Dollár, and C. L. Zitnick (2014). Microsoft COCO: Common objects in context. In *Lecture Notes in Computer Science (including subseries Lecture Notes in Artificial Intelligence and Lecture Notes in Bioinformatics)*, Volume 8693 LNCS, pp. 740–755.

Long, J., E. Shelhamer, O. Vinyals, A. Toshev, S. Bengio, D. Erhan, K. Lenc, A. Vedaldi, E. Denton, S. Chintala, A. Szlam, R. Fergus, P. Fischer, H. Philip, C. Hazırbas, P. V. D. Smagt, D. Cremers, T. Brox, F. Meng, Z. Lu, Z. Tu, H. Li, Q. Liu, V. Mahadevan, and S. Member (2014). Show and Tell: A Neural Image Caption Generator. *arXiv 32*(1), 1–10.

McCarthy, P. M. and S. Jarvis (2010). MTLD, vocd-D, and HD-D: A validation study of sophisticated approaches to lexical diversity assessment. *Behavior Research Methods*.

Papineni, K., S. Roukos, T. Ward, and W. Zhu (2002). BLEU: a method for automatic evaluation of machine translation. *Proceedings of the 40th Annual Meeting on Association for Computational Linguistics* (July), 311–318.

Plummer, B. A., L. Wang, C. M. Cervantes, J. C. Caicedo, J. Hockenmaier, and S. Lazebnik (2017). Flickr30k Entities: Collecting Region-to-Phrase Correspondences for Richer Image-to-Sentence Models. *International Journal of Computer Vision*.

Schuster, S., R. Krishna, A. Chang, L. Fei-Fei, and C. D. Manning (2015). Generating Semantically Precise Scene Graphs from Textual Descriptions for Improved Image Retrieval. *Emnlp*, 70–80.

Senter, R.J.; Smith, E. (1967). Derivation of New Readability Formulas (Automated Readability Index, Fog Count and Flesch Reading Ease Formula) for Navy Enlisted Personnel. Technical report.

Sharif, N., L. White, M. Bennamoun, and S. A. A. Shah (2018). NNEval: Neural network based evaluation metric for image captioning. In *Lecture Notes in Computer Science (including subseries Lecture Notes in Artificial Intelligence and Lecture Notes in Bioinformatics)*, Volume 11212 LNCS.

Teney, D., L. Liu, and A. v. d. Hengel (2016). Graph-Structured Representations for Visual Question Answering. pp. 1–9.

Vedantam, R., C. L. Zitnick, and D. Parikh (2015). CIDEr: Consensus-based image description evaluation. In *Proceedings of the IEEE Computer Society Conference on Computer Vision and Pattern Recognition*, Volume 07-12-June, pp. 4566–4575.

Wu, Q., C. Shen, A. v. d. Hengel, P. Wang, and A. Dick (2016). Image Captioning and Visual Question Answering Based on Attributes and External Knowledge. *IEEE Transactions on Pattern Analysis and Machine Intelligence 40*(6), 1367–1381.

Xu, K., J. L. B. R. Kiros, K. C. A. Courville, and R. S. R. S. Z. Y. Bengio (2016). Show, Attend and Tell: Neural Image Caption Generation with Visual Attention. *IEEE Transactions on Neural Networks 5*(2), 157–166.

Zhu, Y., R. Kiros, R. Zemel, R. Salakhutdinov, R. Urtasun, A. Torralba, and S. Fidler (2015). Aligning books and movies: Towards story-like visual explanations by watching movies and reading books. In *Proceedings of the IEEE International Conference on Computer Vision*, Volume 2015 Inter, pp. 19–27.

Modeling language constructs with fuzzy sets: some approaches, examples and interpretations

Pavlo Kapustin
University of Bergen
pavlo.kapustin@uib.no

Michael Kapustin
Moscow Institute of Physics and Technology
michael.kapustin@gmail.com

Abstract

We present and discuss a couple of approaches, including different types of projections, and some examples, discussing the use of fuzzy sets for modeling meaning of certain types of language constructs. We are mostly focusing on words other than adjectives and linguistic hedges as these categories are the most studied from before. We discuss logical and linguistic interpretations of membership functions. We argue that using fuzzy sets for modeling meaning of words and other natural language constructs, along with situations described with natural language is interesting both from purely linguistic perspective, and also as a meaning representation for problems of computational linguistics and natural language processing.

1 Introduction

The use of fuzzy sets for representing meaning of some types of natural language constructs was first proposed and described in earlier works of Lotfi Zadeh (Zadeh, 1971, 1972). Representation based on fuzzy sets is very expressive as it allows to quantitatively model the nature of the relationship between different concepts, and represent vagueness and imprecision that are so common to natural language.

Nowadays, fuzzy sets seem to be relatively little known among linguists, and little used in natural language processing (Carvalho et al., 2012; Novák, 2017). Most of the examples described in the literature include certain types of adjectives and linguistic hedges.

We would like to contribute to this field by describing a couple of approaches, including different types of projections, that can be used for modeling meaning of some types of language constructs using fuzzy sets. We describe and discuss examples that include some adjectives, adverbs and prepositions. We discuss logical and linguistic interpretations of membership functions (Hersh and Caramazza, 1976), and argue for importance of distinguishing between them when modeling language constructs with fuzzy sets.

2 Related work

Here we briefly mention some of the work related to the use of fuzzy sets as a meaning representation.

In his early works, Lotfi Zadeh suggests modeling meaning of certain types of adjectives (e.g. "small", "medium", "large") as fuzzy sets, and some lingustic hedges (e.g. "very", "slightly" — as operators, acting on these fuzzy sets (Zadeh, 1971, 1972). Hersh and Caramazza (1976) introduce logical and linguistic interpretations of membership functions.

Novák (2017) describes Fuzzy Natural Logic, a mathematical theory that attempts to model semantics of natural language, including Theory of Evaluative Linguistic Expressions (Novák, 2008). Some ways of modeling meaning of words like nouns and verbs) have also been suggested (Novák, 1992, 2017; M. Kapustin and P. Kapustin, 2015). Novák et al. (2016) includes an example of evaluative linguistic expressions that contain perceptions like "near" and "far".

In M. Kapustin and P. Kapustin (2015) we describe a framework for computational interpreting of natural language fragments, and suggest modeling meaning of words as operators. P. Kapustin (2015) describes an application that implements and tests some features of this framework in a simplified setting.

There is some work aiming to make fuzzy sets easier to learn from data. For example, Runkler (2016) describes an approach for generation of linguistically meaningful membership functions from word vectors. We describe compatibility intervals, a meaning representation that is closely related to fuzzy sets (P. Kapustin and M. Kapustin, 2019b).

We discuss how people relate some language constructs to compatibility intervals in an experimental study (P. Kapustin and M. Kapustin, 2019a).

3 Method

3.1 Projections

In this paper, we describe modeling meaning of language constructs by approximating it with a set of *projections* of this construct on different properties (here term "property" is used in a relatively general sense).[1] Each such projection is defined by a fuzzy set and a corresponding membership function that describes compatibility of the construct with different values that the respective property may take. The intuition behind this approach is simple: language constructs contain information about different properties, and information about each property can be modeled as an independent projection.[2]

Consider fig. 1. Presented membership functions attempt to quantitatively relate constructs "expected", "common", "possible", "extraordinary" to surprisingness of a certain result. Of course, meaning of mentioned words is complex and cannot be fully described in terms of surprisingness, but they do tell us something about it, among other things. So, these membership functions may be seen as *projections* of the meanings of these constructs onto property "surprisingness".

3.2 Membership function arguments and values

Regarding values of membership function arguments (in this case, values of "surprisingness"), here we are using a relative scale ranging from zero to one. Choice of scale, including its type (linear, logarithmic, etc.), and mapping between real values and relative values is a topic of separate research and is beyond the scope of this paper.

We look at interpreting membership functions values similarly to Zadeh (1975, 1978): values of membership function can be seen as degrees of compatibility between the value of the function argument and the construct the membership function is describing. Consider fig. 1: $\mu_{\text{expected}}(1) = \mu_{\text{common}}(1) = 0$, because constructs "expected" and "common" are not compatible with high values of surprisingness, and $\mu_{\text{extraordinary}}(1) = 1$, because "extraordinary" is highly compatible with high values of suprisingness (μ is denoting degree of membership).

3.3 Membership functions: different interpretations

Similarly to Hersh and Caramazza (1976), we distinguish between two different interpretations of membership functions: *logical* (modeling what is "logically", or "technically" correct), and *linguistic* (modeling how the word is used).

Consider fig. 2: "young1" corresponds to logical interpretation, reflecting the fact that infants and newborns are, indeed, as young as one can be. On the other hand, "young2" corresponds to linguistic interpretation, reflecting the fact that when people use the word "young", they usually refer to ages other

[1] We propose a related but a bit more specific definition of properties in M. Kapustin and P. Kapustin (2015).

[2] This approach may be seen as a slight generalization of the ideas described in Lotfi Zadeh's early works (Zadeh, 1971, 1972), where construct meaning is modeled as one fuzzy set (one projection), and as a special case of the approach we suggest in M. Kapustin and P. Kapustin (2015), where each concept is modeled as an operator.

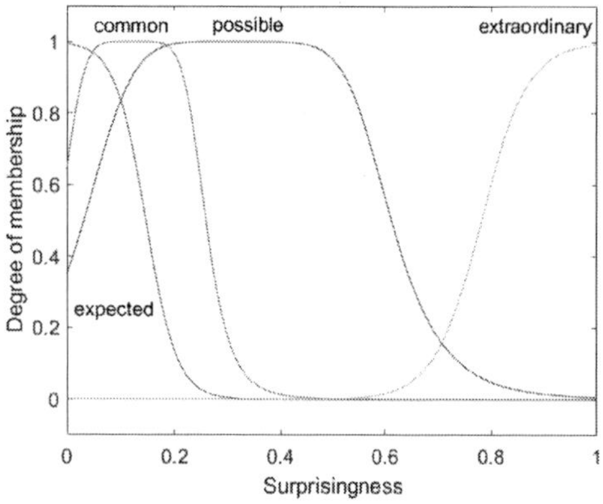

Figure 1: "Expected", "common", "possible", "extraordinary" related to "surprisingness".

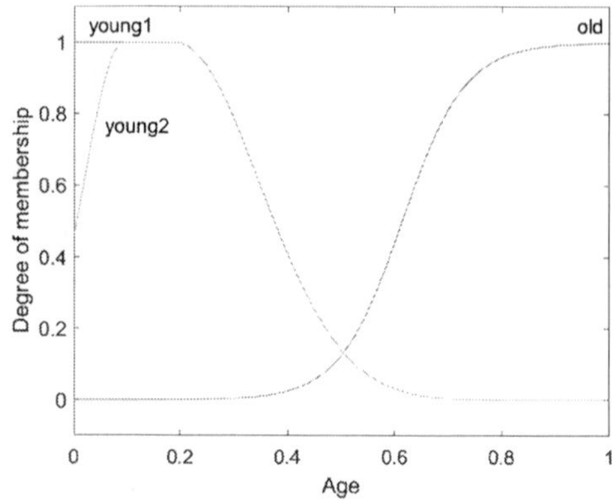

Figure 2: Logical (young1) and linguistic (young2) interpretations.

than newborns and infants. However, for the word "old" its usage does not differ from what is "logically" correct: we may say "old" about someone who is 80 or 100 years old.

Let's consider fig. 1 again: $\mu_{\text{expected}}(0) > \mu_{\text{common}}(0) > \mu_{\text{possible}}(0)$. This corresponds to linguistic interpretation and models that, even though highly anticipated results are probably both common and possible, "expected" might be a better word than "common" (and especially than "possible") to describe such results (of course, this only takes "surprisingness" into account).

We believe that many, but probably, not all of the differences between logical and linguistic interpretations are related to scalar implicatures and related phenomena, and believe that this needs to be investigated further.

Differing logical and linguistic interpretations have some interesting implications. Consider fig. 3. Here we apply negation, implemented as Zadeh's complementation (Zadeh, 1972), to constructs "young1", "young2" and "old". While such negation seems to work well with the logical interpretation, it gives somewhat unexpected results with the linguistic interpretation: according to $not(\mu_{\text{young2}})$, it appears that infants are less "not young" than newborns, which is not correct.

We think that logical and linguistic interpretations complement each other, each of them modeling different aspects of the meaning of the language constructs, and for some words may need to be modeled as separate membership functions. Examples in this paper follow linguistic interpretation (unless mentioned otherwise).

3.4 Choice of constructs, projections and membership functions

The choice of constructs, projections and membership functions in this paper is subjective and serves as an illustration. For the experimental study, please see P. Kapustin and M. Kapustin (2019a).

4 One-dimensional projections

One-dimensional projection is a projection onto one property that allows to model how a language construct relates to this property.

4.1 One-dimensional projections: time references

Here we describe how one-dimensional projections can be used for modeling meaning of words like "after", "afterwards", "later", "until" and "since". In these examples we choose to focus on the meaning

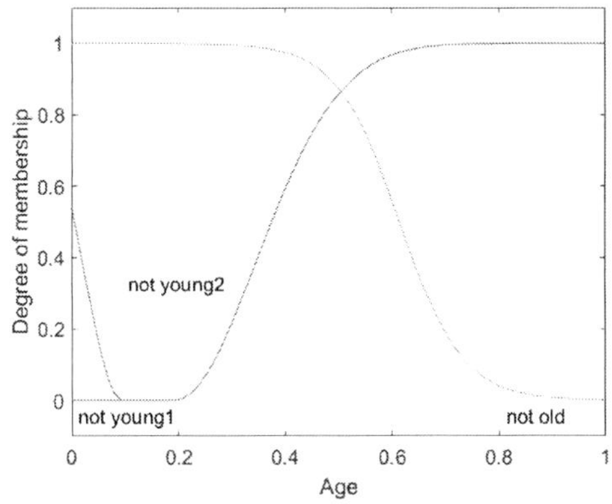

Figure 3: Negation of young2 gives somewhat unexpected results.

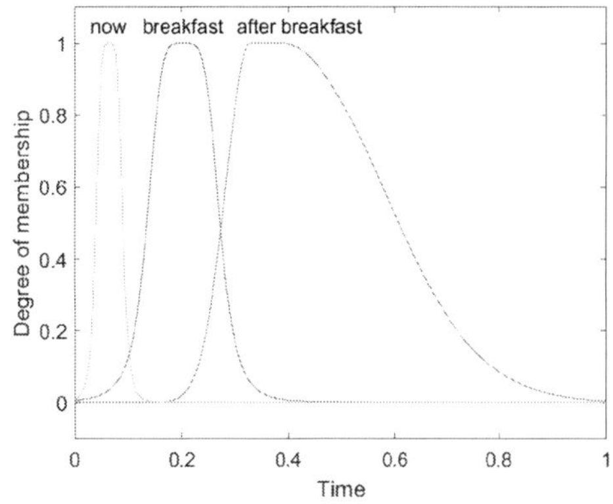

Figure 4: Time reference given by "after breakfast" in "you can play after breakfast".

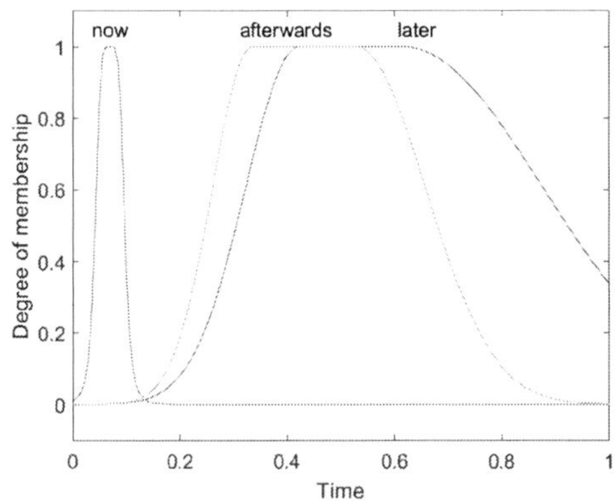

Figure 5: Time references given by "afterwards" and "later" in "let's discuss this afterwards / later".

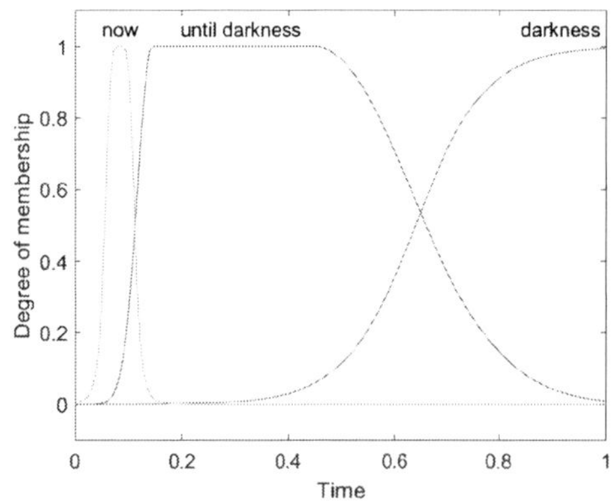

Figure 6: Time references given by "until darkness" in "you can play until darkness".

aspect of the words that has to do with providing a time reference relative to the time of utterance (given by "now").

Consider fig. 4. Here we choose to model "after" as suggested by Vocabulary.com (2018a): "happening at a time subsequent to a reference time", that's why the membership function for "after breakfast" is decreasing relatively rapidly (this would be different if we chose to model "after" as in "the world has changed after the Second World War"). "Before" may be modeled in a similar way, but we do not include a figure here for brevity.

Consider fig. 5. Here we choose to model "afterwards" as a function that decreases relatively rapidly after a certain point, agreeing with dictionaries mentioning that a certain reference time is usually assumed (Vocabulary.com, 2018b; Cambridge.org, 2018a). On the other hand, "later" is modeled as "at some time in the future" (Vocabulary.com, 2018c; Cambridge.org, 2018b), that's why the function is decreasing slower, $\mu_{\text{later}} > \mu_{\text{afterwards}}$ in more distant future, and $\mu_{\text{later}}(1) > 0$. This would be different if we chose to model "later" as a synonym for "afterwards" (this meaning of "later" is also suggested by the same dictionaries).

Consider figs. 6 and 7. The fact that the time references given by "darkness" and "summer" are relatively vague is modeled by slow decrease of $\mu_{\text{untilDarkness}}$ and slow increase of $\mu_{\text{sinceSummer}}$.

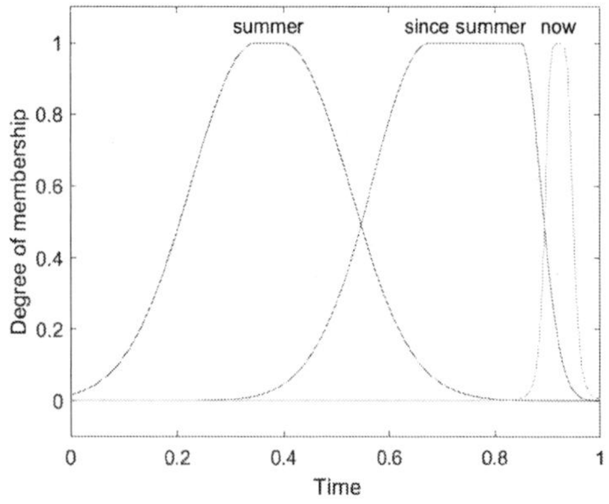

Figure 7: Time reference given by "since summer" in "you have had the book since summer".

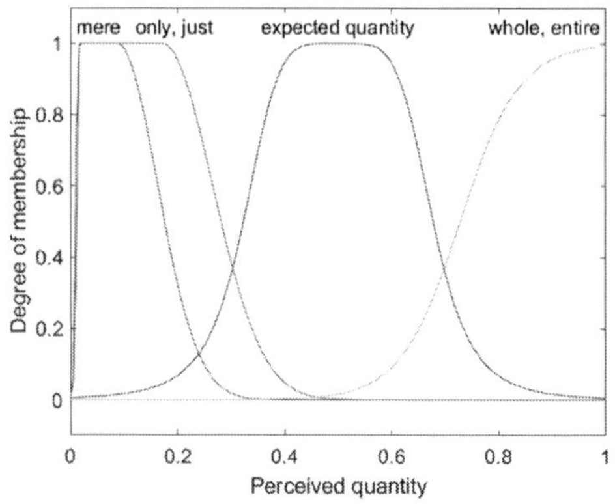

Figure 8: "Mere", "only", "just", "whole", "entire" related to perceived quantity in "only two days", "whole room", "mere one percent".

4.2 One-dimensional projections: perception of quantities

Consider fig. 8. Here we suggest how one-dimensional projections can be used to model meaning of words like "only", "just", "whole", "entire", "mere". In these examples we choose to focus on what these words tell us about certain quantity compared to our expectations (e.g. Zeevat, 2009; Berkeley.edu, 2019). We use name "perceived quantity" for the property.

Here we let $\mu_{\text{whole}}(1) = \mu_{\text{entire}}(1) = 1$ to model the fact that words "whole" and "entire" may be used with something perceived as very large (e.g. "entire universe"). On the other hand, we let $\mu_{\text{mere}}(0) = \mu_{\text{only}}(0) = \mu_{\text{just}}(0) = 0$, because we cannot think of examples when these words are used with zero quantities (e.g. "a mere zero", "only nothing" and "just no one" sound strange). Also, here we choose to model "mere" as a more specific word than "only" and "just", as suggested by OxfordDictionaries.com (2019b): "used to emphasize how small or insignificant someone or something is". Here we do it by letting μ_{mere} cover less area than $\mu_{\text{only, just}}$ on fig. 8.

4.3 One-dimensional projections on related properties: repeating events

Consider fig. 9. Here we are attempting to model what the words "seldom", "occasionally", "regularly", "often" tell us about event frequency (as in "I often play chess"). The words "occasionally" and "regularly" seem to be less specific than the words "seldom" and "often", and we model this by letting their membership functions cover larger area under the curve.

Consider fig. 10, where we are attempting to model what the words "seldom", "occasionally", "regularly", "usually", "often" tell us about expectedness of an event (as in "I often play chess when we meet with my friends")[3]. We model "regularly" as a more specific word on fig. 10 than on fig. 9, because we believe that "I regularly play chess when I meet with my friends" means a rather high expectedness of the game of chess if the meeting happens (but lower than for "usually" or "often").[4] Note that we include "usually" on fig. 10, but not on fig. 9, because it is possible to say "I usually play chess when I meet with my friends", while "I usually play chess" sounds strange.

In this example words "seldom", "occasionally", "regularly", "often" have two independent projections on related properties: "frequency" and "expectedness". In general, we think that having multiple independent projections on related properties is interesting, in particular because it may help the systems

[3] Here by "expectedness" we mean "the quality or state of being expected" (CollinsDictionary.com, 2019).

[4] We discuss how people relate these and other constructs to compatibility intervals (P. Kapustin and M. Kapustin, 2019b), a representation closely related to fuzzy sets, in an experimental study (P. Kapustin and M. Kapustin, 2019a).

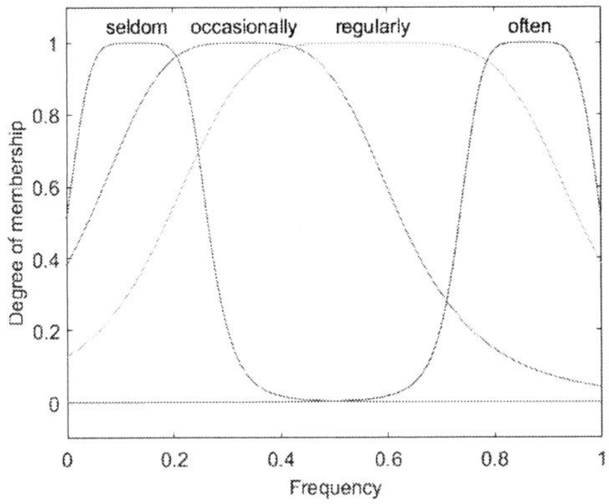

Figure 9: "Seldom", "occasionally", "regularly", "often" related to event frequency.

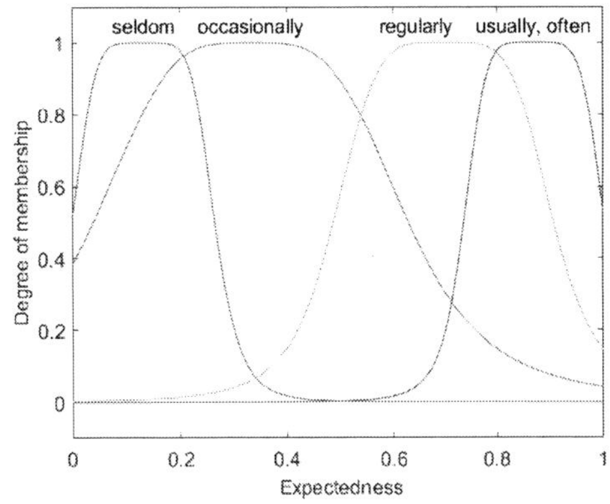

Figure 10: "Seldom", "occasionally", "regularly", "usually", "often" related to event expectedness.

learn more about the relation between these properties, and needs more research.

5 Membership functions that depend on other functions

5.1 Membership functions that depend on other functions: sufficiency and excess

Consider figs. 11 and 12. Here we are attempting to model what constructs "enough", "not enough", and "too much" tell us about the amount of certain property with respect to how much property is desirable/acceptable, modeled with a separate desarability/acceptability function.[5] We believe that for the construct "not enough" to be meaningful, there should be a place where desirability/acceptability function is increasing (e.g. "not enough air pollution" usually does not make sense). Likewise, the construct "too much" (or too expensive, etc.) only makes sense if there is a place where desirability/acceptability function is decreasing (e.g. "I have too much money" would often require an explanation to answer why having less money would be more desirable).

Here we follow linguistic interpretation for μ_{enough}, modeling the fact that we would normally use words other than "enough", when the amount of property is much higher than the amount qualifying as "enough", and that is why μ_{enough} is gradually decreasing after a certain point. We let $\mu_{\text{enough}}(1) > 0$ as "enough" may still be used in such situations (e.g. "he earns enough" may be used about a millionaire when one prefers to be less specific).

It is interesting to note that figs. 11 and 12 present examples when both membership functions and the scale of members function arguments depend on another function (in this case, desirability / acceptability). We believe that such dependencies need further research for such models to become practically useful for problems of computational linguistics and natural language processing.

6 Multi-dimensional projections

Sometimes modeling meaning of certain constructs requires membership functions that take several arguments, when it is the relation of the arguments is what defines the concept. Here we are discussing several examples of this kind.

Consider figs. 13 and 14. Like many other constructs, "already" and "still" have several related meanings with subtle differences. Here we are focusing on modeling surprise at the fact that something happens or will happen earlier or later than expected (e.g. Zeevat, 2009, 2013; Cambridge.org, 2019a,

[5]Similar notion of admissibility is used in Meier (2003).

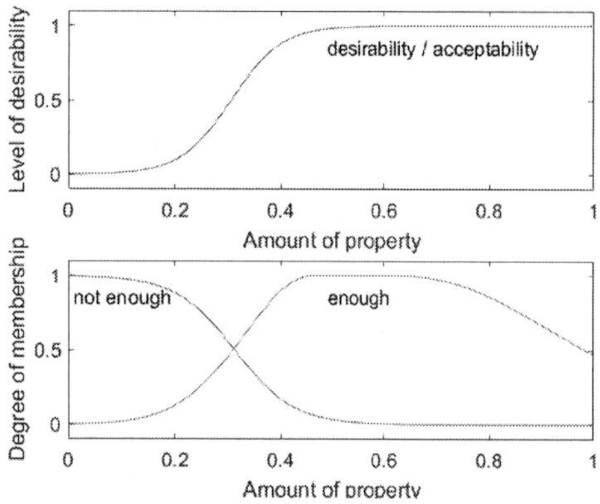

Figure 11: "Enough" and "not enough" related to the amount of property in "enough / not enough for everyone".

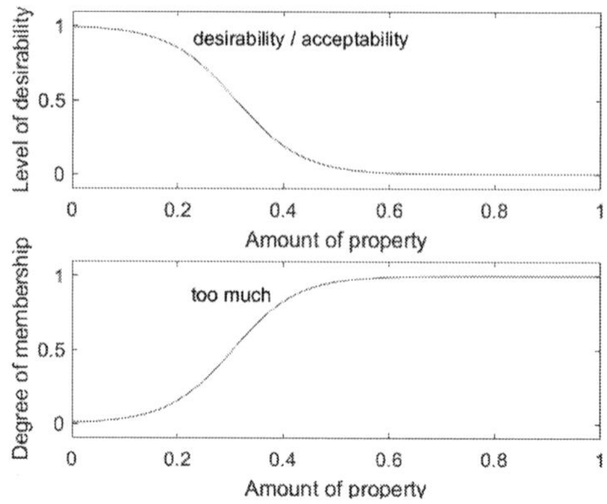

Figure 12: "Too" related to the amount of property in "I think that owning a car is too expensive these days".

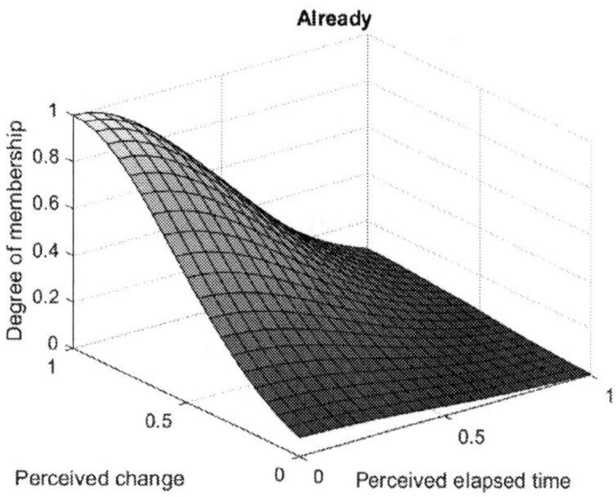

Figure 13: "Already" related to perceived change and perceived elapsed time in "it is already finished".

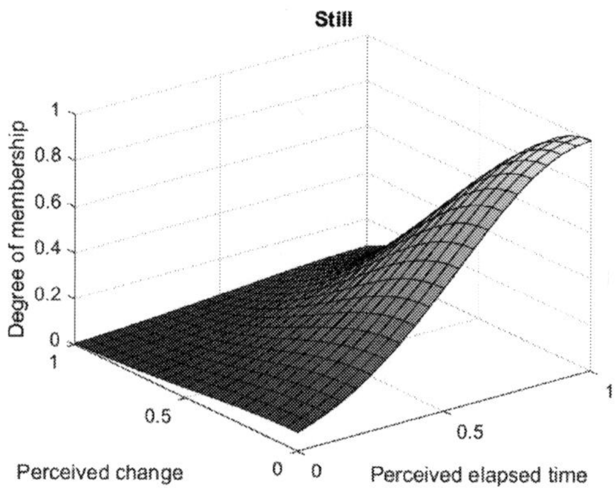

Figure 14: "Still" related to perceived change and perceived elapsed time in "they are still working".

2019d). We represent these constructs by relating properties "perceived change" and "perceived elapsed time". "Already" means that perceived elapsed time is relatively low, and perceived change is relatively high, while "still" means the opposite.

Consider fig. 15. Here we model construct "efficient" by relating properties "progress" and "elapsed time": "efficient" means that elapsed time is relatively low, and progress is relatively high.

Consider fig. 16. Many dictionaries define "lately" as "recently" or "not long ago" (OxfordDictionaries.com, 2019a; Cambridge.org, 2019c; Merriam-Webster.com, 2019). However, Cambridge.org (2019b) explains that "lately" is used for states or repeating events, mostly with present perfect, and is not used for single events. Here we choose to model "lately" in this meaning, as a word that describes recent state of things: when the time is close to zero (further in the past), pretty much all states are compatible with the construct "it rains a lot lately". In other words, we have no information about the state of things, and this is modeled by membership degree of "lately" being approximately equal to one, as long as time is close to zero. When the time is closer to one (recent past), only the states with high average rainfall are compatible with the construct. It seems that "lately" is sometimes used as a word that contrasts recent situation with earlier situation, however we believe that this can be very context dependent, and choose not to model it here: according to fig. 16, we don't know how things were in the past.

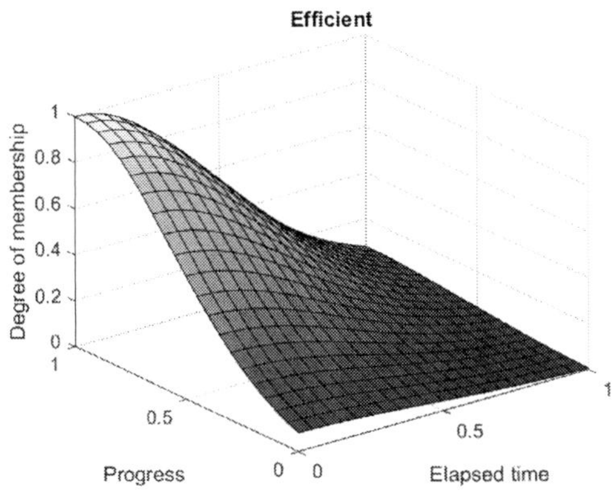

Figure 15: "Efficient" related to progress and time in "this dryer is very efficient".

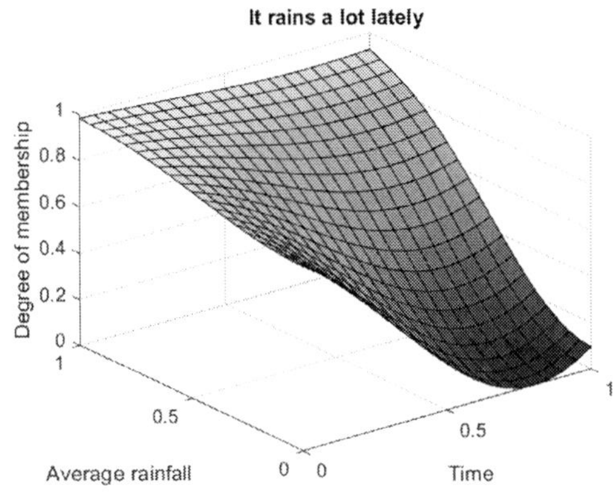

Figure 16: "Lately" related to time and average rainfall in "it rains a lot lately".

7 Discussion

Although the choice of membership functions used in the examples is subjective, we hope that they are a useful illustration to the approaches and ideas described in the paper, as well as to the importance of distinguishing between logical and linguistic interpretations of membership functions. For the experimental study, please see P. Kapustin and M. Kapustin (2019a).

One can see applications of such models both in natural language understanding and natural language generation. When a system meets a language construct, it can understand it in terms of "underlying" properties, e.g. "often" — in terms of "frequency", and "already" — in terms of the relation between "perceived change" and "perceived elapsed time". Similarly, having information about possible values of property or properties, a system can attempt to describe the situation with appropriate words, e.g. information about "progress" and "time" can be described using words like "efficient".[6]

We think that wider adoption of fuzzy sets in computational linguistics and natural language processing may benefit from the research that will help to make such models easier to learn from data. For example, Runkler (2016) describes an approach for generation of linguistically meaningful membership functions from word vectors. We suggest a meaning representation that is closely related to membership functions, but may be somewhat easier to learn from data (P. Kapustin and M. Kapustin, 2019b).

In many cases, when trying to understand how the membership functions should behave, and even qualitatively compare membership functions for related words, it was not that easy to find linguistic evidence in the literature. In some cases we had a feeling that dictionary definitions left some important parts of the construct meaning unexplained (but it was clear from the examples or explanations found elsewhere). We noticed these things because of our attempts to model meanings of the constructs in a more formal way (in this case using membership functions).

We argue that fuzzy sets and membership functions are useful tools that are interesting both from purely linguistic perspective, and also as a meaning representation for problems of computational linguistics and natural language processing, and hope that more researchers become interested in this area.

Acknowledgements

We thank Vadim Kimmelman and Csaba Veres for helpful discussions and comments. We thank anonymous reviewers for helpful feedback.

[6]We suggest one approach for describing situations in words in M. Kapustin and P. Kapustin (2015).

References

Berkeley.edu (2019). Frame:RankedExpectation. https://framenet2.icsi.berkeley.edu/fnReports/data/frameIndex.xml?frame=Ranked_expectation.

Cambridge.org (2018a). Afterwards. https://dictionary.cambridge.org/dictionary/english/afterwards.

Cambridge.org (2018b). Later. https://dictionary.cambridge.org/dictionary/english/later.

Cambridge.org (2019a). Already. https://dictionary.cambridge.org/grammar/british-grammar/already.

Cambridge.org (2019b). Late or lately. https://dictionary.cambridge.org/grammar/british-grammar/late-or-lately.

Cambridge.org (2019c). Lately. https://dictionary.cambridge.org/dictionary/english/lately.

Cambridge.org (2019d). Still. https://dictionary.cambridge.org/grammar/british-grammar/still.

Carvalho, J. P., F. Batista, and L. Coheur (2012). A critical survey on the use of fuzzy sets in speech and natural language processing. In *Fuzzy Systems (FUZZ-IEEE), 2012 IEEE International Conference on,* 1–8. IEEE.

CollinsDictionary.com (2019). Expectedness. https://www.collinsdictionary.com/dictionary/english/expectedness.

Hersh, H. M., and A. Caramazza (1976). A fuzzy set approach to modifiers and vagueness in natural language. *Journal of Experimental Psychology: General* 105 (3): 254.

Kapustin, M., and P. Kapustin (2015). Modeling meaning: computational interpreting and understanding of natural language fragments. *arXiv preprint arXiv:1505.08149.*

Kapustin, P. (2015). Computational comprehension of spatial directions expressed in natural language. Master's thesis, The University of Bergen.

Kapustin, P., and M. Kapustin (2019a). Language constructs as compatibility intervals: an experimental study. In preparation.

Kapustin, P., and M. Kapustin (2019b). Modeling meaning of language constructs using compatibility intervals. In submission.

Meier, C. (2003). The meaning of too, enough, and so... that. *Natural Language Semantics* 11 (1): 69–107.

Merriam-Webster.com (2019). Lately. https://www.merriam-webster.com/dictionary/lately.

Novák, V. (1992). The alternative mathematical model of linguistic semantics and pragmatics. In *The Alternative Mathematical Model of Linguistic Semantics and Pragmatics,* 87–183. Springer.

Novák, V. (2008). A comprehensive theory of trichotomous evaluative linguistic expressions. *Fuzzy Sets and Systems* 159 (22): 2939–2969.

Novák, V. (2017). Fuzzy logic in natural language processing. In *Fuzzy Systems (FUZZ-IEEE), 2017 IEEE International Conference on,* 1–6. IEEE.

Novák, V., I. Perfilieva, A. Dvorák, et al. (2016). *Insight into Fuzzy Modeling.* John Wiley & Sons.

OxfordDictionaries.com (2019a). Lately. https://en.oxforddictionaries.com/definition/lately.

OxfordDictionaries.com (2019b). Mere. https://en.oxforddictionaries.com/definition/mere.

Runkler, T. A. (2016). Generation of linguistic membership functions from word vectors. In *Fuzzy Systems (FUZZ-IEEE), 2016 IEEE International Conference on,* 993–999. IEEE.

Vocabulary.com (2018a). After. https://www.vocabulary.com/dictionary/after.

Vocabulary.com (2018b). Afterwards. https://www.vocabulary.com/dictionary/afterwards.

Vocabulary.com (2018c). Later. https://www.vocabulary.com/dictionary/later.

Zadeh, L. A. (1971). Quantitative fuzzy semantics. *Information Sciences* 3 (2): 159–176.

Zadeh, L. A. (1972). A Fuzzy-Set-Theoretic Interpretation of Linguistic Hedges. *Journal of Cybernetics.*

Zadeh, L. A. (1975). The concept of a linguistic variable and its application to approximate reasoning—I. *Information sciences* 8 (3): 199–249.

Zadeh, L. A. (1978). Fuzzy sets as a basis for a theory of possibility. *Fuzzy sets and systems* 1 (1): 3–28.

Zeevat, H. (2009). "Only" as a mirative particle.

Zeevat, H. (2013). Expressing surprise by particles. In *Beyond Expressives: Explorations in Use-Conditional Meaning,* 297–320. Brill.

Topological Data Analysis for Discourse Semantics?

Ketki Savle
UNC Charlotte
kropleka@uncc.edu

Wlodek Zadrozny
UNC Charlotte
wzadrozn@uncc.edu

Minwoo Lee
UNC Charlotte
Minwoo.Lee@uncc.edu

Abstract

In this paper we present new results on applying topological data analysis (TDA) to discourse structures. We show that topological information, extracted from the relationships between sentences, can be used in inference, namely it can be applied to the very difficult legal entailment problem given in the COLIEE 2018 data set. Previous results of Doshi and Zadrozny (2018) and Gholizadeh et al. (2018) show that topological features are useful for classification. The applications of computational topology to entailment are novel, and in our view provide a new set of tools for discourse semantics: computational topology can perhaps provide a bridge between the brittleness of logic and the regression of neural networks. We discuss the advantages and disadvantages of using topological information, and some open problems such as explainability of the classifier decisions.

1 Introduction

Topology is a classic branch of mathematics that deals with shape invariants such as the presence and numbers of holes. More recently *topological data analysis* (TDA) was introduced as a branch of computational mathematics and data science, predicated on the observation that data points have implicit shapes (e.g. Edelsbrunner and Harer (2010)). Throughout the paper we will be using the word *topology* only in these two particular senses.

Both topology and TDA can be viewed as an abstraction mechanism, where we replace the original shape or cloud of data points by some numbers representing their mathematical properties, using a formal machinery derived from algebraic topology. In case of TDA, we use software implementing these methods.

A natural question to ask is whether texts or discourse structures have shapes that can be measured using tools of topology. Zhu (2013) was the first to investigate this question and observed we can capture some information about discourse structures using topological structures, namely homological persistence (which we do not have space to define here, and we simply use it as a source of numerical features). Zhu used a collection of nursery rhymes to illustrate how topology can be used to find certain patterns of repetition. More recently, Doshi and Zadrozny (2018) applied Zhu's method in a larger setting showing its classification superiority on the task of assigning movie genres to user generated plot summaries, using the IMDB data set. They improved on the early 2018 state of the art results of Hoang (2018), which was achieved using deep learning on this large data set. Gholizadeh et al. (2018) applied a different method for computing homological persistence to the task of authorship attribution, which is also a classification task, showing that the patterns of how authors introduce characters in novels can be captured to large extent using topological descriptors. Interestingly, neither of these works uses topological features to augments the usual tf/idf representations of documents: Doshi and Zadrozny (2018) use counts of words (from a previously identified vocabularies) to form a matrix which is the only input to topological persistence, and then they make a rule based decision based only on the presence of barcodes; and Gholizadeh et al. (2018) use time series. To use topological data analysis (TDA), Zhu (2013) assumes that text is implicitly coherent (SIFTS method), and so do Doshi and Zadrozny (2018). Namely, they assume implicit connection between consecutive sentences in each document. While for movie plots this assumption makes sense, it might be more problematic in other contexts, such as entailment, especially when two passages are unrelated.

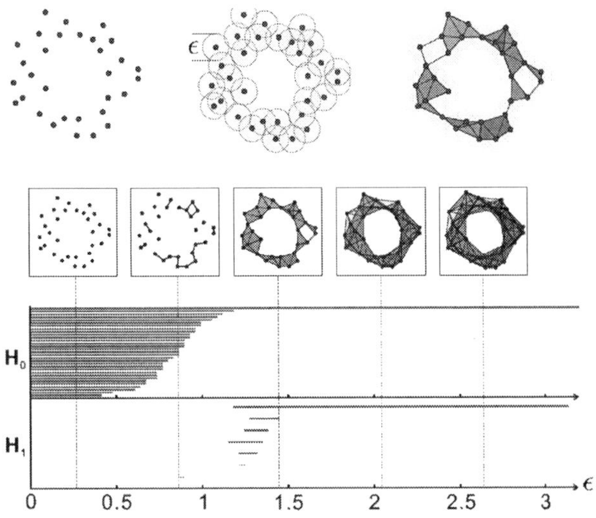

Figure 1: Persistence homology is a data analysis tool. Intuitively, as we start expanding the data points into balls of increased radii, planar figures emerge and change. The intervals in H_0 and H_1 capture relevant features of this process, namely the number of connected components, and the number of holes at different resolutions. The method abstracts distance information about the feature vectors of original data. It is an open problem how exactly these new numerical features help entailment. Source of the figure: Huang et al. (2018)

1.1 Our results

In this paper, we present our very recent results on applying topological data analysis (TDA) to entailment, with some improvement of accuracy over the baseline without persistence.

More specifically, this paper shows TDA works on entailment improving the task of classification for establishing entailment on the COLIEE 2018 task by over 5% (F-measure) compared to the results classification without topology that is using only tf/idf and similarity. Furthermore, this result does not assume the existence of the implicit skeleton connecting consecutive sentences (as was done in Doshi and Zadrozny (2018), following Zhu (2013)).

The title of the present article ends with a question mark. This question mark reflects the tension between the positive empirical results derived using topological methods and our lack of understanding why these methods work. Thus, perhaps another contribution of this paper is to point to both, the need for theoretical inquiry about relationships between discourse and its topological abstractions, and more importantly to the need for tools that would allow us to experiment with such hypothetical relations. As we speculate in Section 4, the effectiveness of TDA for entailment *might* be explainable using the known mathematical connections of topology and logic (e.g. Vickers (1996)). Proper tooling could prove or disprove this hypothesis.

1.2 A minimum background on topological data analysis

Topological Data Analysis (TDA) can be viewed as a method of data analysis done at different resolutions. Informally speaking, this process can be viewed as data compression(cf. Lum et al. (2013)). It can also be viewed as an attempt to reconstruct shape invariants, such as presence of voids or holes, from collection of points, at different resolutions (Edelsbrunner et al. (2000)). Or in yet another formulation TDA tries to make data points fit together, and measures their divergence from perfect fit Robinson (2014) (we will not be using this last property here).

Figure 1 (taken from Huang et al. (2018)) conveys these ideas: it shows a cloud of data points, and its subsequent approximation by balls of increased radii. The overlaps produce a change in shape which can be measured using the H_0 and H_1 lines: The number of H_0 lines intersecting the vertical bar at ϵ is the number of connected components of when the points are extended with balls of that radius. Therefore as

ϵ increases, the number of components decreases. In this process the exact values of the data points are ignored, but the shape information is preserved – that is, two clouds of similar shapes but different values will have similar persistence diagrams. The H_1 lines show the birth and death of holes at given values of ϵ. The top line show a hole persisting from 1.2 to 3.3 (approximately). Jointly, H_0 and H_1 (and higher H_n's , not discussed here) compress information about the shape of the point cloud. This diagram deals only with planar structures, but persistence works in higher dimensions as well, in principle allowing machines to "see" shapes in dimensions higher than 3, a task difficult for humans. "Persistence" refers to the fact that the number of components and holes remains stable at some intervals, and we record this fact as numerical features; "homology" means similarity (of shape).

In NLP, the points are in a high dimensional space and represent vectors of tf/idf or other features derived from text. The method works the same, but *please note that Figure 1 only illustrates how TDA progresses from points to shapes. At this point, we do not know — and we see it as a major open problem — what aspects of natural language semantics, whether for entailment or classification, are captured by topological features.*(Although, as mentioned earlier, some aspects of this problem are discussed in Zhu (2013)).

To finish this introduction, we mention an equivalent representation, called *persistence diagram*, an example of which appears later in Figure 5, represents birth and death as two dimensional coordinates, and uses colors to make a distinction between H_0 and H_1. To repeat, the representation method is general, and it generates numbers we can use as machine learning features. However, finding the corresponding natural language mechanisms responsible for the improvements in accuracy of classification or entailment is an open problem.

1.3 Related work on applying topological data analysis to discourse modeling, and text processing in general

Applications of TDA to text started with discourse: Zhu (2013) used nursery rhymes to illustrate properties of homological persistence (e.g. that it is not simply measuring repetitions), and also showed that children, adolescent and adult writing styles can be differentiated using TDA. Doshi and Zadrozny (2018) used Zhu's tools and methods to show that topological features can improve the accuracy of classification (movie plots). They also discuss the paucity of applications of TDA to text, and the fact that not all of these applications show improvements over the state of the art: in particular this was the case for sentiment analysis and clustering Michel et al. (2017). Temčinas (2018) argues for applicability of persistent homology to lexical analysis using word embeddings, and in particular for discovery of homonyms such as 'bank', thus potentially for word sense disambiguation.

For discourse analysis, broadly speaking, we see that according to Guan et al. (2016) TDA can help with extraction of multiword expressions and in summarization; also it might be worth to mention Horak et al. (2009) apply TDA to a networks of emails, but without going into their text. In other words, TDA for text data is an emerging area of research, perhaps with a potential to be of value for computational linguistics (see the last two sections of this paper for an additional discussion).

2 Entailment between legal documents

The COLIEE task: Our application of topological data analysis (TDA) to computing entailment focuses on the legal entailment COLIEE [1] task, i..e *Competition of Legal Information Extraction and Entailment (COLIEE).*

To solve an entailment task, given a decision of *a base case*, along with its summary and facts, the system should be able to establish the relation of entailment with an associated *noticed case*, given as a list of paragraphs. We can define it as, given a base case b, and its decision d, and another case r represented by its paragraphs $P = \{p_1, p_2, p_3, \ldots, p_n\}$, and we need to find the set $E =$

[1]COLIEE 2018 Workshop collocated with JURISIN 2018: `https://sites.ualberta.ca/~miyoung2/COLIEE2018/`

$\{p_1, p_2, \ldots, p_m \mid p_i \in P\}$, where $entails(p_i, d)$ denotes a relationship which is true when $p_i \in P$ entails the decision d (c.f. Rabelo et al. (2018), Kim et al. (2016), Adebayo et al. (2016)).

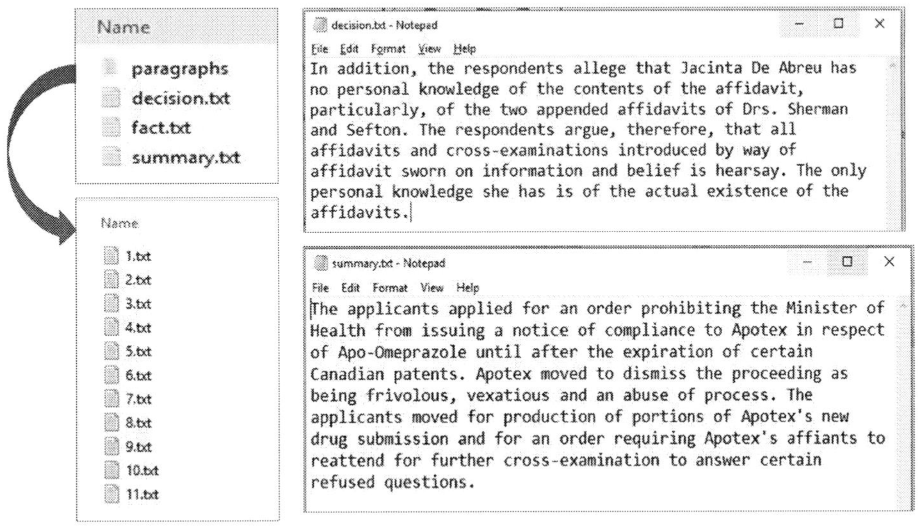

Figure 2: Each case folder includes decision file, summary file and fact file with paragraph folders. Decision file is an actual query i.e. a decision of a base case, summary file consists of a summary of a base case and facts file includes all the human annotated facts about the base case.

Text	Hypothesis
As previously stated, the applicant contends that the CRDD based its decision that his testimony lacked credibility or trustworthiness by drawing inferences unsupported by the evidence and by ignoring portions of the applicant's testimony and documentary evidence A Convention refugee claimant applied for judicial review of the dismissal of his claim by the Convention Refugee Determination Division of the Immigration and Refugee Board.	It is my opinion that the Board acted arbitrarily in choosing without valid reasons, to doubt the applicant's credibility concerning the sworn statements made by him and referred to supra. When an applicant swears to the truth of certain allegations, this creates a presumption that those allegations are true unless there be reason to doubt their truthfulness. See: Villaroel v. M.E.I. (1979), 31 N.R. 50, and more particularly footnote number 6 to the Reasons of Pratte, J. On this record, I am unable to discover valid reasons for the Board doubting the truth of the applicant's allegations above referred to.

Figure 3: Above example illustrates entailment between text and hypothesis for one of the base cases of COLIEE 2018. Text column consists of decision and summary of a base case and the hypothesis is an entailed supporting paragraph for a given base case. (We have excluded facts file in text while demonstrating as size of its text is large)

Overview of dataset: For training, there were 181 base cases provided which were drawn from an existing collection of Federal Court of Canada law cases. Every case consists of a decision file, summary file, facts file and a list of paragraph files. The training data also consists of labels in XML format for entailed paragraphs. Our task was to identify paragraphs from this list, that entails with the decision of a base case. In 181 base cases, the number of paragraph files were 8794 out of which 239 were positively entailed and the rest were not entailed. This led us to a very imbalanced class ratio of 2.71% examples in positive class and 97.29 % in negative class.

Why this task is difficult: Since the data is of legal domain, it might require an understanding of law to analyze it: A traditional approach such as training neural network, or the more intuitive semantic similarity approach did not work very well on this dataset. Reason being, pre-trained word embedding such as GloVe and word2vec may not contain enough legal terms for neural networks to learn. Similarity correlates with entailment, but it clearly is a different problem. Also, this corpus is too small to use it to create our own pre-trained word embeddings. And at this point we do not have the bandwidth to pursue corpus expansion and create appropriate legal embeddings. An example of the type of text present in the COLIEE data is shown in Fig.3.

Another challenge was data distribution. Using common re-sampling techniques for classification task along with tf/idf leads to predicting always the negative class and treating positive class as noise, giving false high accuracy.

The best results obtained on COLIEE leaderboard was of Rabelo et al. (2018) where they employed similarity-based feature vector and used a "candidate" paragraph, chosen from histogram of the similarities between each noticed case and all paragraphs for classification. In this method, due to the unstructured input format, their team used post processing for classifier's predictions. In case of too many positive detections, they retained 5 candidate paragraphs whereas for zero positive predictions they retained 1 paragraph by choosing classifier's confidence interval. With this approach they delivered 0.24 precision, 0.28 recall and 0.26 F-score.

3 Computing entailment with and without topological features

To see whether topological features provide any additional information we employed a supervised machine learning approach. We represented the data points as a set of elements of type "[text, hypothesis], Label". We defined "text" as a combination of decision file, summary file, and fact file; and "hypothesis" as a list of paragraphs for a case. For cleaning the text data, we simply removed punctuation, stop-words followed by converting the text to lower case and stemming it. This process, together and the features used in the experiments are shown in Fig. 4.

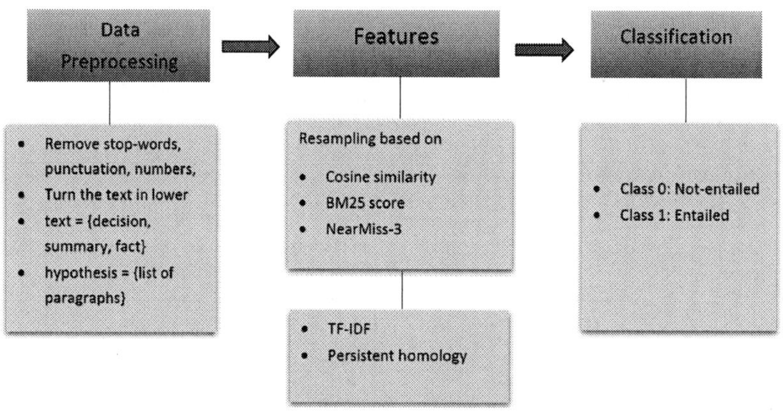

Figure 4: Diagram represents pipeline used for establishing entailment. A simple flow was to pre-process the data, prune highly similar and relevant paragraphs and resample further using NearMiss-3, then in the second pass, use homology features along with tf/idf.

We then formulated the problem as a binary classification problem for establishing corresponding paragraphs as entailed or not entailed with a base case. Mathematically, given a training data $D = (x_i, y_i)$ for $i = 1, ..., N$, where $x_i = \{texts, hypothesis\}$, and $y_i = \{0, 1\}$.

3.1 Method 1: Relevance and similarity approach.

Considering every case had a list of paragraphs and severe imbalance, we approached this problem by first ranking the paragraph files using Okapi BM25 algorithm. We also calculated cosine similarity of a text and its hypothesis, and combined these features to re-sample the data, which we hoped would maximize the probability of establishing entailment without any information loss. Using the augmented samples that are highly relevant and similar with the base case, we computed TF-IDF vectors using `sklearn`. To retain the order of a sequence of every sentence we used n-gram range hyper-parameter with value 1 to 3. This experiment was performed using Random Forest classifier for binary classification. The results, shown in Table 1 show improvement over previously reported top score of Rabelo et al. (2018) – note, however, our results were obtained after the JURISIN 2018 competition. Our main point was to see whether topological features provide additional value.

3.2 Method 2: Topological Data Analysis approach.

We wanted to examine if topology could create stronger signals to capture entailment. From the previous method we learned that entailment cannot be explained by establishing similarity only. By measuring the distance between two documents, one cannot necessarily infer a meaning of one text from another. In Information Retrieval, if a document is relevant to a given query, it does not necessarily mean that the meaning of a query can be completely inferred from the retrieved document. In fact, this creates a need for entailment in various NLP tasks including IR.

We used *Ripser*, a C++ library to compute persistent homology, for establishing topological structure of documents.[2] Ripser was applied both to text and hypothesis. Our assumption is if text is entailed with hypothesis then the corresponding values of birth, death radius can provide stronger signals to the classifier. Unlike the movie classification experiment, we did not observe any specific barcode structure for entailed and non-entailed paragraphs, but the radius of birth-death cycle was significantly different for entailed documents as compared to the non-entailed ones. Another reason for not having a specific structure between such documents could be the length of these documents, as each file consists of 5 sentences on an average. In future we aim to perform this experiment on larger size documents to see if there is any obvious barcode structure between entailed documents, and that can visually give us a clear interpretation.

After calculating homology, we combined persistent homology features with tf/idf to create a feature vector comprised of the same. We used Random Forest classifier for binary classification task to establish entailment. Notably, we have not assumed the existence of coherence skeletons in documents (SIFTS in Zhu (2013)).

Experiment and Results:

We used tenfold cross-validation, setting a random sample of 22 cases aside from given 181 cases for the evaluation task. From our first method where we used highly similar and relevant paragraphs for classification along with tf/idf feature vector, our best results were 0.28 precision score, 0.58 recall and 0.38 F-score for entailed class (see Table 1).[3] We improved our precision score by 2.5%, recall by over 14% and F-score by over 5% using topological data analysis. (Our aim was to achieve higher F-score for classification other than recall as a naïve implementation can give 1.0 recall by predicting all paragraphs as entailed). Using topological features, we could see reduction in predicting false positives, and more accurate predictions for true positives. We experimented with three machine learning classifiers out of which we obtained the best results using Random Forest.

[2] `https://github.com/Ripser/ripser`

[3] These results were obtained after the COLIEE competition.

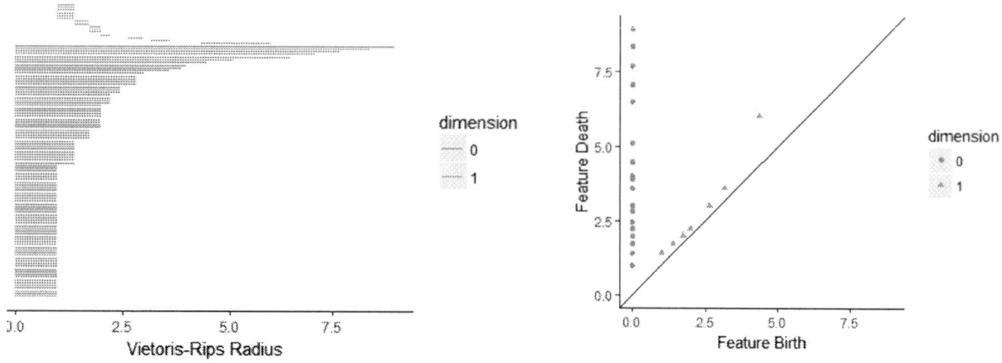

Figure 5: Left Panel: Barcode structure of persistent homology capturing multiple cycles. Note the the differences in radius of one long cycle and the others. Right panel: Persistent diagram representing the cycles from the left panel. Note the dot further from the diagonal corresponding to the long cycle. We show that these cycles are informative (Table 1), but we do not have tools to understand precisely how.

Method	**Precision**	**Recall**	**F-score**
Robelo et al. (2018) [prior art]	24%	28%	26%
Similarity + relevance score + tf/idf+ RF	28.2	58.3	37.6
Similarity + relevance score + tf/idf + RF + **Topology**	30.7	72.5	**43.0**

Table 1: Results of the classification experiments using Random Forest (RF) with 10-fold validation; RF produced best results, with and without topological features. In the first experiment, using proper filtering and resampling improved the F-score compared with COLIEE 2018 prior art. More importantly, we see that *the presence of topological features is informative for entailment* – this is the main point of the paper.

4 Discussion and Open Problems

As shown in Table 1, the use of topological features, namely birth-death information shown in Fig. 5, can improve the accuracy of computing entailment. However, it is an open issue to understand what exactly is being captured by using persistence. This can be seen as two sets of open problems: (a) we do not know exactly the correspondence between text and homological features; (b) we do not have instruments to capture these relationships.

We understand these relationship on some the abstract, mathematical level, even for text; in Zhu (2013) and Doshi and Zadrozny (2018) experiments, because of the simple setups, the 1-dimensional persistence measures the tie backs of content words. However, this is less clear for entailment, and we do not have instruments that would allow us to go back from the classifier decision and show the meaning of the topological features in documents we were using. *Thus the abstract and concrete explainability of topological text features is an open problem.* In addition, as the referees observed, entailment has direction, but distances used by our out of the box TDA methods are symmetric. So, what *exactly* is happening? – We don't know. However, asymmetric structures as in Fig. 1 can arise from (symmetric) distances between points. One hypothesis we plan to explore is that "global alignment" of Dagan et al. (2010) is captured by homological persistence. Similarly, it is conceivable that feature inclusion measures such as `APinc`, `balAPinc` , see e.g. Baroni et al. (2012), are indirectly captured by homological persistence. Again, it is an open problem what exactly is happening here.

In principle asymmetric measures of distance can be used in computational topology, see: Bubenik and Vergili (2018) and also discussion in Hennig and Liao (2013). Whether doing so would help entailment is an open problem.

To continue with speculations, there is a category theoretical style of research on entailment and distributional semantics, e.g. Bankova et al. (2016). There are also deep connections between topology, category theory and logic (e.g. Vickers (1996)). And we could even add physics to the mix: Baez and

Stay (2010). Given the connections between intuitionistic logic, Heyting algebras and topology, and the possibility of translation between these three representations (Vickers (1996)), we can speculate if we properly do computational topology for inference, we should get approximately-correct intuitionistic, logical inference methods. This could be an important connection, since logics are proverbially brittle, and computational topology is not. Thus our results *might* be experimentally confirming this intuition, and on a pretty difficult data set.

5 Summary and Conclusion

TDA can be computationally expensive, as observed by many researchers, and also Huang et al. (2018) to argue that quantum computing methods might be appropriate (if they materialize). However topological features seem to provide advantage when only small amount of the data is available, as shown here, and also in Doshi and Zadrozny (2018), who used only small percentage of data for preparation and training. This is also the case in our related work (Savle and Zadrozny (2019)), where we improved on Doshi and Zadrozny (2018) movie plot classifcation results by changing the inputs to the computation of persistent homologies from binary matrices to tf/idf representations augmented with persistence, which is the representation used here. Furthermore, we did not use the assumption of time skeleton Zhu (2013). From discourse interpretation point of view, this shows the assumption of discourse coherence does not have to be built in into the TDA method. But, again, the trade-offs between these two approaches are unclear.

Similarly, if larger amounts of data are given (e.g. movie plots), the precise computational tradoffs between using topology versus deep neural networks are unclear, especially given the ongoing improvements on various text analysis benchmarks, and new methods for addressing these tasks appearing on a daily basis.

Our future work includes, in the near horizon, experimenting with other data sets, possibly using graph embeddings in addition to topology. In a slightly longer horizon, we also want to explore higher dimensional persistence, which was shown in Horak et al. (2009) to capture relevant properties of a social network (email exchanges), but has not, to our knowledge, been used for other aspects of discourse understanding. And in parallel, we will be focusing on building tools to help us answer the question what exactly is captured by topological features.

In summary, this work confirms the ability of topological features to effectively capture certain structural properties of discourse text. On the one hand, it is another application of topological data analysis to text. On the other hand, given the paucity of positive results in this space (as discussed in the Introduction), and no previously reported applications to inference, we see our work as giving a new tool for computational discourse semantics, which could be used, as we have shown, as an addition to existing tools. Therefore, in our view, this research opens a new area of discourse analysis, where regression-based tools (such as standard machine learning and neural networks) can be used jointly with structural tools: to logic and ontology we can therefore add topology. From a formal point of view, with the known correspondence between intuitionistic logic and topology, the effectiveness of computational topology for inference, should yield approximate (and mostly correct) inference methods. This work shows that indeed this might possible, even for relatively difficult cases of entailment.

Acknowledgments: We thank the referees of IWCS 2019 for their comments and suggested improvements. Most of the issue raised by them we addressed in the preceding section. Unfortunately, explaining why exactly topological methods work on entailment is an open problem.

Authors' contributions: K. Savle designed, ran and analyzed the results of the experiments under the guidance of W. Zadrozny, and with additional help from M. Lee, esp. in analyzing machine learning results. KS and WZ were the primary writers of this paper.

References

Adebayo, K. J., L. Di Caro, G. Boella, and C. Bartolini (2016). TEAMNORMAS's participation at the coliee 2016 bar legal exam competition, (submission id: N01). In *Tenth International Workshop on Juris-informatics (JURISIN)*.

Baez, J. and M. Stay (2010). Physics, topology, logic and computation: a rosetta stone. In *New structures for physics*, pp. 95–172. Springer.

Bankova, D., B. Coecke, M. Lewis, and D. Marsden (2016). Graded entailment for compositional distributional semantics. *arXiv preprint arXiv:1601.04908.*

Baroni, M., R. Bernardi, N.-Q. Do, and C.-c. Shan (2012). Entailment above the word level in distributional semantics. In *Proceedings of the 13th Conference of the European Chapter of the Association for Computational Linguistics*, pp. 23–32. Association for Computational Linguistics.

Bubenik, P. and T. Vergili (2018). Topological spaces of persistence modules and their properties. *Journal of Applied and Computational Topology*, 1–37.

Dagan, I., B. Dolan, B. Magnini, and D. Roth (2010). Recognizing textual entailment: Rational, evaluation and approaches–erratum. *Natural Language Engineering 16*(1), 105–105.

Doshi, P. and W. Zadrozny (2018). Movie genre detection using topological data analysis and simple discourse features. In *Proc. 6th International Conference on Statistical Language and Speech Processing, SLSP 2018, Vol. 11171 of Lecture Notes in Computer Science, Springer.*

Edelsbrunner, H. and J. Harer (2010). *Computational topology: an introduction.* American Mathematical Soc.

Edelsbrunner, H., D. Letscher, and A. Zomorodian (2000). Topological persistence and simplification. In *Foundations of Computer Science, 2000. Proceedings. 41st Annual Symposium on*, pp. 454–463. IEEE.

Gholizadeh, S., A. Seyeditabari, and W. Zadrozny (2018). Topological signature of 19th century novelists: Persistent homology in text mining. *Big Data and Cognitive Computing* 2(4), 33.

Guan, H., W. Tang, H. Krim, J. Keiser, A. Rindos, and R. Sazdanovic (2016). A topological collapse for document summarization. In *Signal Processing Advances in Wireless Communications (SPAWC), 2016 IEEE 17th International Workshop on*, pp. 1–5. IEEE.

Hennig, C. and T. F. Liao (2013). How to find an appropriate clustering for mixed-type variables with application to socio-economic stratification. *Journal of the Royal Statistical Society: Series C (Applied Statistics) 62*(3), 309–369.

Hoang, Q. (2018). Predicting movie genres based on plot summaries. *arXiv preprint arXiv:1801.04813.*

Horak, D., S. Maletić, and M. Rajković (2009). Persistent homology of complex networks. *Journal of Statistical Mechanics: Theory and Experiment 2009*(03), P03034.

Huang, H.-L., X.-L. Wang, P. P. Rohde, Y.-H. Luo, Y.-W. Zhao, C. Liu, L. Li, N.-L. Liu, C.-Y. Lu, and J.-W. Pan (2018). Demonstration of topological data analysis on a quantum processor. *Optica 5*(2), 193–198.

Kim, M.-Y., R. Goebel, Y. Kano, and K. Satoh (2016). Coliee-2016: evaluation of the competition on legal information extraction and entailment. In *International Workshop on Juris-informatics (JURISIN 2016).*

Lum, P. Y., G. Singh, A. Lehman, T. Ishkanov, M. Vejdemo-Johansson, M. Alagappan, J. Carlsson, and G. Carlsson (2013). Extracting insights from the shape of complex data using topology. *Scientific reports 3*, srep01236.

Michel, P., A. Ravichander, and S. Rijhwani (2017). Does the geometry of word embeddings help document classification? a case study on persistent homology based representations. *arXiv preprint arXiv:1705.10900*.

Rabelo, J., M.-Y. Kim, H. Babikar, R. Goebel, and N. Farruque (2018). Information extraction and entailment for statute law and case law. In *JURISIN 2018*. Available at http://research.nii.ac.jp/jurisin2018/.

Robinson, M. (2014). *Topological signal processing*. Springer.

Savle, K. and W. Zadrozny (2019). Topological data analysis for text classification. *under review*.

Temčinas, T. (2018). Local homology of word embeddings. *arXiv preprint arXiv:1810.10136*.

Vickers, S. (1996). *Topology via logic*, Volume 5. Cambridge University Press.

Zhu, X. (2013). Persistent homology: An introduction and a new text representation for natural language processing. In *IJCAI*, pp. 1953–1959.

Semantic Frame Embeddings for Detecting Relations between Software Requirements

Waad Alhoshan, Riza Batista-Navarro and Liping Zhao
School of Computer Science
University of Manchester
Oxford Road, Manchester M13 9PL, UK

Abstract

The early phases of requirements engineering (RE) deal with a vast amount of software requirements (i.e.,requirements that define characteristics of software systems), which are typically expressed in natural language. Analysing such unstructured requirements, usually obtained from stakeholders' inputs, is considered a challenging task due to the inherent ambiguity and inconsistency of natural language. To support such a task, methods based on natural language processing (NLP) can be employed. One of the more recent advances in NLP is the use of word embeddings for capturing contextual information, which can then be applied in word analogy tasks. In this paper, we describe a new resource, i.e., embedding-based representations of semantic frames in FrameNet, which was developed to support the detection of relations between software requirements. Our embeddings, which encapsulate contextual information at the semantic frame level, were trained on a large corpus of requirements (i.e., a collection of more than three million mobile application reviews). The similarity between these frame embeddings is then used as a basis for detecting semantic relatedness between software requirements. Compared with existing resources underpinned by frame embeddings built upon pre-trained vectors, our proposed frame embeddings obtained better performance against judgments of an RE expert. These encouraging results demonstrate the potential of the resource in supporting RE analysis tasks (e.g., traceability), which we plan to investigate as part of our immediate future work.

1 Introduction

As a part of Requirements Engineering (RE), requirements analysis is "a critical task in software development as it involves investigating and learning about the problem domain in order to develop a better understanding of stakeholders actual goals, needs, and expectations" (Hull et al., 2017). However, it is a challenge to analyse requirements to find relations between them, especially implicit ones, i.e., those that are not expressed explicitly and formally, especially within a lengthy document. As stated by Ferrari et al. (2017), these challenges are mainly due to the semantic ambiguity and incompleteness inherent to natural language. Moreover, performing an RE analysis task, e.g. by manually inspecting words and implicit or explicit relations between requirements, is a time-consuming and error-prone procedure (Fernández et al., 2017).

One of the approaches that has drawn the attention of the RE research community is semantic analysis. Representing under-specified meanings within requirements in a structured manner will lead to a more efficient way for conducting RE analysis task. As an example, Mahmoud and Niu (2015) discussed the importance of using techniques for measuring semantic relatedness in tracing links (or relations) between requirements. This mimics the human mental model in understanding links between pieces of text through their implicit meanings. Natural language processing (NLP) tools and techniques offer viable solutions to many tasks in RE, including requirements analysis (Dalpiaz et al., 2018). However, the majority of the available NLP techniques and resources are not domain-specific, i.e., they are trained or built based on general-domain data sets (e.g., news articles). For this reason, a recent research direction in RE calls for "customizing general NLP techniques to make them applicable for solving the problems requirements engineers face in their daily practice" (Ferrari et al., 2017).

In this work, we present a new resource, i.e., semantic frame embeddings, built upon semantic frames in FrameNet (Baker et al., 1998). To demonstrate an application to requirements analysis, we employed our semantic frame embeddings in computing semantic relatedness between software requirements at a semantic frame level.

The rest of this paper is organised as follows: Section 2 provides background information on FrameNet and word embeddings, while Section 3 presents the method we carried out to generate the frame embeddings. In Section 4, we discuss the results of employing the obtained frame embeddings in a semantic relatedness measurement task. Finally, we conclude and briefly discuss our ongoing work in Section 5.

2 Background

2.1 A Brief Overview on FrameNet

Fillmore (1976) proposed the linguistic theory of semantic frames, stating that each word in a language is accompanied by essential knowledge which is important to understand its full meaning. For example, words such as "store" and "keep" are usually accompanied by the following elements: (1) an agent that performs a storing event; (2) an object which is a result of the storing event; and (3) the location where the object is kept.

FrameNet[1] is a web-based general-domain semantic lexicon that implements the semantic frame theory. Initially started by Baker et al. (1998), it has continued to grow and now contains more than 1,200 semantic frames (Baker, 2017). For every semantic frame in FrameNet, the following information is given: frame title, definition, frame elements and lexical units (LUs). LUs are words that evoke the frame, represented as a combination of their lemmatised form and part-of-speech (POS) tag. The concept of keeping an object, for example, which is stored in FrameNet as a semantic frame entitled *Storing* is evoked by the LU *save.v* where *v* stands for verb, among other LUs. Its core frame elements, which are essential in understanding the meaning of the frame, include Agent, Location and Theme. FrameNet also catalogues non-core frame elements which are used to enhance the understanding of a specific frame. For the *Storing* frame, Manner, Duration, and Explanation are considered as non-core elements.

In Figure 1, we demonstrate the use of semantic frames and their related LUs for representing a set of software requirements. From the given example in Figure 1, we can identify the requirements and conditions for implementing the designated system, e.g., accessing restrictions to the documents as shown in in Req-1 and Req-2. The need to update records on a regular basis as described in Req-3 and Req-4 are also shown. These requirements are abstractly represented by using FrameNet frames. For instance, accessing restrictions are represented by the *Deny_or_grant_permission* and *Preventing_or_letting* frames from FrameNet. Similarly, the processed materials "reports", "logs", and "contact information" are captured by the *Text*, *Records* and *Information* frames, respectively.

Furthermore, some frames (e.g., *Storing*, *Records*, *Verification*, and *Frequency*) are repeated amongst the requirements in Figure 1, boosting the semantic relatedness between these requirements. FrameNet holds a representation of semantic relations between its frames (Baker, 2017). For example, the frame *Record* inherits from the *Text* frame. Using such semantic relations could help create links between annotated requirements, as reported in our previous work Alhoshan et al. (2018c). However, according to Baker (2017) not all frames in FrameNet are semantically connected. For example, *Information* and *Records* are not linked in any way. Similarly, *Deny_or_grant_permission* and *Prenveting_or_letting* are not connected in FrameNet although both frames share some LUs (e.g., *permit.v*). For this reason, rather than rely on the semantic relations encoded in FrameNet, we sought another way to find semantic links between FrameNet frames.

[1]https://framenet.icsi.berkeley.edu/

Req-1: The transaction records are kept into a central database of the Bank and only authorised users are able to view the documents.

FN-Req-1: The transaction **records** [*Records*] are **kept** [*Storing*] into a central database of the Bank and only **authorised** [*Deny_or_grant_permission*] users are **able** [*Capability*] to **view** [*Perception_active*] the **documents** [*Text*].

Req-2: The Bank's reports are stored and restricted i.e. accessing the logs should be allowed to specific users.

FN-Req-2: The Bank's **reports** [*Text*] are **stored** [*Storing*] and **restricted** [*Deny_or_grant_permission*] i.e. accessing the **logs** [*Records*] should be **allowed** [*Preventing_or_letting*] to **specific** [*Specific_individual*] users.

Req-3: The Bank's clients are requested to confirm their personal information regularly.

FN-Req-3: The Bank's clients are **requested** [*Request*] to **confirm** [*Verification*] their personal **information** [*Information*] **regularly** [*Frequency*].

Req-4: Every year the bank control systems shall ask the clients to verify their contact information.

FN-Req-4: **Every** [*Frequency*] **year** [*Calendric_unit*] the bank **control** [*Being_in_control*] **system** [System] shall **ask** [*Request*] the clients to **verify** [*Verification*] their **contact** [*Contacting*] **information** [*Information*].

Figure 1: A set of software requirements, where "Req" refers to the raw requirements and "FN-Req" refers to the requirements annotated with FrameNet frames titles (highlighted with colours) and their evoked LUs (in bold font).

2.2 Word Embeddings

One of the recent advances in NLP research is the use of word embeddings as a method for capturing the context of any given word in a corpus of documents. According to Mikolov et al. (2013), word embeddings allow words with similar, or related meanings, to have similar vector representations. They are learned based on the principle of distributional semantics, which posits that words occurring in the same context have similar or related meanings (Harris, 1954). Deep learning offers a framework for representing word context as real-valued vectors, that goes beyond the counting of co-occurrences and takes into account word order as well (Bengio et al., 2003). For training word embeddings, a large and representative corpus is needed. There are existing pre-trained, general-domain word embeddings ready for use, e.g., the Word2Vec embeddings trained on 100 billion words from Google News (Mikolov et al., 2013).

In general, word embeddings have helped boost the performance of various NLP tasks. An example is word analagy, where word embeddings provide the capability to calculate semantic similarities between words (Fu et al., 2014). However, the use of word embeddings can lead to even better performance if they are trained on corpora specific to the domain of interest or application. This could potentially reduce the problem of out-of-vocabulary (OOV) words (Jozefowicz et al., 2016), i.e., the lack or sparsity of instances of certain words in the training corpus, which leads to not being able to capture or map their context in embedding vectors. The solution to such cases is typically based on simply ignoring the OOV words, which is not ideal.

In this work, we proposed a solution for mitigating text sparsity that is based on semantic frames. Rather than mapping each word in the text, we target a group of words which represent a semantic frame, hence producing *semantic frame embeddings*. There are previously reported efforts that proposed the use of frame embeddings, e.g., Sikos and Padó (2018) and Alhoshan et al. (2018c). In our work, we aim to develop frame embeddings that are suitable for captruing the context of RE-related documents.

3 Semantic Frame Embeddings

Our method for generating frame embeddings was previously discussed in our prior work Alhoshan et al. (2018c) which we employed existing word embeddings developed by Efstathiou et al. (2018). In this paper, we trained our own word embeddings which then formed the basis for generating semantic frame embeddings. Afterwards, we measured the semantic relatedness between frames using different similarity metrics. Finally, we selected the most suitable metric for applying frame embeddings to the RE domain.

3.1 Preparation of Training Data

As a first step, we generated a corpus of requirements documents that are more similar to software requirements, i.e., a collection of user reviews of mobile applications. Using the web-based AppFollow tool[2], reviews from different mobile application repositories (e.g., Apple Store and Google Play) were retrieved. The user reviews covered different categories of mobile applications, i.e., business, sports, health, travel, technology, security, games, music, photos, videos, shopping, lifestyle, books, social networking, finance. While each review came with metadata such as review date, title and per-user application rating, we took into consideration only the textual content of the reviews. This resulted in a total of 3,019,385 unique reviews/documents in our training data set.

The documents in the training data set were then preprocessed with the following steps: sentence splitting, tokenisation, stop-word removal, part-of-speech (POS) tagging and lemmatisation. The preprocessing results allowed us to automatically check for the occurrence of LUs (associated with semantic frames) catalogued in FrameNet, in order to assess the data set's coverage of semantic frames. Based on this, we were able to determine that our mobile application reviews data set covers all of the 123 semantic frames annotated in FN-RE corpus (a FrameNet annotated corpus of software requirements presented in Alhoshan et al. (2018a,b).

3.2 Training Word Embeddings

Utilising the preprocessed mobile application reviews data set as a corpus, we trained word embeddings using the continuous bag-of-words (CBOW) learning method of *Word2Vec* as proposed by Mikolov et al. (2013). A word embedding vector was trained for each LU, which was represented as a combination of its lemmatised form and POS tag. Taking into account the POS tag of an LU makes it possible to train different vectors for words with the same lemma but different parts of speech. It is preferable, for example, to train a vector for "form" as a verb (*form.v*) that is different from the vector for "form" as a noun (*form.n*). The size of each vector was set to 300, following previously reported work in Sikos and Padó (2018) and Mikolov et al. (2013).

3.3 Generating Frame Embeddings

The word embedding vectors resulting from the previous step were then used to form an embedding-based representation of semantic frames, i.e., *frame embeddings*. That is, for any given semantic frame F, we collected the vectors corresponding to the LUs that evoke it. The average of these LU vectors is then computed and taken as the frame embedding for F. For instance, as 11 LUs are associated with the *Creating* frame in FrameNet, a vector containing the average over the 11 word embedding vectors corresponding to these LUs was obtained as part of this step.

3.4 Measuring Frame-to-Frame Semantic Relatedness

The generated frame embeddings were employed in computing relatedness between semantic frames. Following our method described in Alhoshan et al. (2018c), we used the cosine similarity metric. For

[2]https://appfollow.io

FrameNet frames *X* and *Y*, let *FR(X,Y)* denote the relatedness between these two frames:

$$FR_{Cosine}(X,Y) = \frac{\mathbf{F_X} \cdot \mathbf{F_Y}}{\|\mathbf{F_X}\|\|\mathbf{F_Y}\|} \tag{1}$$

where $\mathbf{F_X}$ and $\mathbf{F_Y}$ are the frame embedding vectors for *X* and *Y*, respectively.

The cosine similarity metric measures the angle between two vectors (i.e., frame embeddings). If the vectors are close to parallel (e.g., with $R(X,Y) \approx 1$) then we consider the frames as similar, whereas if the vectors are orthogonal (i.e., with $R(X,Y) \approx 0$), then we can say that the frames are not related.
In addition, we used two other similarity metrics, Euclidean Distance and Manhattan Distance, for later comparison:

$$FR_{Euclidean}(X,Y) = \sqrt{(\mathbf{Fx} - \mathbf{Fy})^2} \tag{2}$$

$$FR_{Manhattan}(X,Y) = \|\mathbf{Fx} - \mathbf{Fy}\| \tag{3}$$

Similar to the cosine metric, the Euclidean and Manhattan metrics measure the distance between two data points (i.e., distance between the two frame embeddings) to detect their similarity—i.e., if the data points are close together (with a shorter distance), this is considered as a higher similarity between the designated frame embeddings to be measured.

The Manhattan distance metric calculates the path between any two data points as it would be placed in a grid-like path, whereas the Euclidean distance measures the distance as a straight-line.

An issue that is related to the distance scores of both Euclidean and Manhattan metrics is that the results can be too large (i.e., greater than 1) if the data points to be compared are sparse. For this reason, we applied the Z_{score} in order to normalise obtained results from Euclidean and Manhattan distance metrics separately:

$$Z_{score}(Fx, Fy) = \frac{Dxy - \mu}{\alpha} \tag{4}$$

Z_{score} is a function for normalising Dxy which is the similarity distance calculated by FR between *Fx* and *Fy* (calculated using either Euclidean or Manhattan distance) where μ is the mean distance over all frame pairs, and α is the standard deviation.

For implementing the methods described above, we employed various Python-based packages. The preprocessing pipeline was implemented using the NLTK Python package[3] as well as NodeBox[4]. Meanwhile, the Word2Vec implementation available in the Gensim package[5] facilitated the training of word embeddings. The numpy package[6] was used in generating the frame embeddings and calculating similarity scores, and matplotlib [7] for visualising the frame embeddings relations.

4 Results

In this section, we discuss the results obtained by using the frame embeddings generated by the method described above. We used the 123 semantic frames in FrameNet that are annotated in the FN-RE corpus, reported in Alhoshan et al. (2018b). The first author of this paper, who is a PhD candidate investigating the use of NLP techniques in RE, annotated the semantic relatedness between the selected frames pairs as "yes" if the frame pair is semantically related according to their definition and related (or shared) LUs, and "no" otherwise.

We applied the three similarity metrics discussed in Section 3.4, on the frame embeddings of the selected frame pairs as exemplified in Table 1. The results obtained from Euclidean and Manhattan

[3]https://www.nltk.org/

[4]https://www.nodebox.net/code/index.php/Linguistics

[5]https://radimrehurek.com/gensim/models/word2vec.html

[6]http://www.numpy.org/

[7]https://matplotlib.org/

distance metrics are normalised according to our discussion above. We considered 0.50 as a threshold value to indicate semantic relatedness for any frame pair in the set, following prior work by Alhoshan et al. (2018c). From the given results in Table 1, it is clear that using the cosine metric provides more reliable relatedness scores that are close to the registered human-judgement—i.e., out of six positive scores of semantic relatedness on the given frame pairs shown in Table 1, the cosine metric identified five of them as semantically related with scores that are equal or higher than the used minimum threshold value. The cosine metric is generally used to identify semantic relatedness regardless of the magnitude of the frame embedding, whereas both the Euclidean and Manhattan metric measure the actual magnitude distance between the frame embeddings. For example, the frame *Sending* occurs 0.824% in the training corpus and the frame *Receiving* occurs only 0.007% of the time. The Euclidean and Manhattan metrics measure the similarity of these two frames depending on how often they occurred in the corpus, whereas cosine similarity measures only the angle of their vector representations. For this reason, we selected the cosine metric to compare our frame embeddings with the pre-trained frame embeddings.

Table 1: Results of frame pair semantic relatedness scores according to the applied similarity metrics. Underlined values pertain to the highest valued score (above the minimum threshold) for each semantically related frame pair.

Frames Pairs	**Human-judgements: Semantically related?**	**Euclidean Distance (Normalised)**	**Manhattan Distance (Normalised)**	**Cosine similarity**
(Sending, Creating)	**Yes**	<u>0.8622</u>	-0.6653	0.5794
(Sending, Intentionally_create)	**Yes**	-0.6249	-0.62574	<u>0.5383</u>
(Sending, Receiving)	**Yes**	-0.3409	-0.3443	<u>0.5356</u>
(Sending, Recording)	No	-0.2469	-0.2050	0.4538
(Creating, Intentionally_create)	**Yes**	-1.3837	-1.3967	<u>0.9034</u>
(Creating, Receiving)	No	-0.3098	-0.3406	0.4697
(Creating, Recording)	No	-0.3329	-0.3422	0.4573
(Intentionally_create, Receiving)	No	-0.2057	-0.2170	0.3703
(Intentionally_create, Recording)	Yes	-0.2570	-0.2769	0.3778
(Receiving, Recording)	**Yes**	-0.1992	-0.2102	<u>0.5081</u>

In Table 2, we compare the characteristics of the frame embeddings based on word embeddings pre-trained on news articles as used by Sikos and Padó (2018) (Column A), those pre-trained on Stack-overflow posts by Efstathiou et al. (2018) used in Alhoshan et al. (2018c) (Column B), and our own proposed embeddings (Column C).

Table 2: Comparison between our proposed Frame Embeddings (C) and the two available frame embeddings (A) and (B).

Feature	**FrameNet Corpus Frame Embedding (A)**	**FN-RE Corpus Frame Embedding version 1.0 (B)**	**FN-RE Corpus Frame Embedding version 2.0 (C)**
Trained data set size	31.0 MB	1.5 GB	990.1 MB
data set context	News articles	Stack overflow technical posts User	reviews of mobile applications
Number of words entries	21,121 words	1.7 million words	1.6 million words
Language Model	Word2Vec (dimension size: 300)	Word2Vec (dimension size: 200)	Word2Vec (dimension size: 300)
Context	General	Software Engineering	Requirements Engineering

The frame embeddings (A) and (B) are compared with our proposed frame embeddings (C) based on a data set of frame pairs whose semantic relatedness has been labelled. The results are shown in Table 3. For example, *Creating* and *Intentionally_create* frames, have some LUs in common (e.g., *create.v*, *generate.v* and *make.v*). Both frames are connected via the inheritance relation *is-a* in FrameNet.

During the annotation of the FN-RE corpus, described in Alhoshan et al. (2018a) and Alhoshan et al. (2018b), those two frames (*Creating* and *Intentionally_create*) in particular are overlapping and describe very similar contexts. As shown in Table 3, the frame pair *(Creating, Intentionally_create)* obtained a significant relatedness score of 0.903 according to our frame embeddings (C). More importantly, our frame embeddings provided overall semantic relatedness results that are closer to our judgement, as we discussed previously in this section. Such encouraging results indicate that using a training corpus that is specific to the RE context provides improved results.

Table 3: Semantic relatedness scores (computed using cosine similarity) for each frame pair according to our proposed frame embeddings (C) and the two other frame emebeddings (A) and (B). Underlined values pertain to the highest score (above the minimum threshold) for each semantically related frame pair.

Compared Frames Pairs	**Human-judgments: Semantically related?**	**General FrameNet Corpus Frame (A)**	**FN-RE Corpus Frame Embedding version 1.0 (B)**	**FN-RE Corpus Frame Embedding version 2.0 (C)**
(Sending, Creating)	**Yes**	0.2642	0.3722	<u>0.5795</u>
(Sending, Intentionally_create)	**Yes**	0.2320	0.4175	<u>0.5383</u>
(Sending, Receiving)	**Yes**	0.2605	<u>0.6466</u>	0.5356
(Sending, Recording)	No	0.2356	0.5587	0.4538
(Creating, Intentionally_create)	**Yes**	0.8318	0.4338	<u>0.9034</u>
(Creating, Receiving)	No	0.3433	0.2677	0.4697
(Creating, Recording)	No	0.3084	0.2508	0.4573
(Intentionally_create, Receiving)	No	0.3008	0.3496	0.3703
(Intentionally_create, Recording)	Yes	0.3620	0.2867	0.3778
(Receiving, Recording)	**Yes**	0.2722	0.2875	<u>0.5081</u>

As shown in previous work, semantic frames are a promising means for capturing the meaning of software requirements ,e.g., Alhoshan et al. (2018c). Our encouraging results demonstrate that with careful selection of a similarity metric (for measuring semantic relatedness) and a suitable training data set representing software requirements, our proposed semantic resource (i.e., the frame embeddings) combines the strengths of semantic frames and embedding-based representations– which can be integrated with RE tools to support the task of software requirements analysis and traceability.

5 Conclusion

We presented a novel language resource to aid in finding semantic relations between software requirements, in support of RE tasks. The proposed resource is based on the development of an embedding-based representation of semantic frames in FrameNet (i.e., frame embeddings), trained on a large corpus of user requirements, consisting of more than three million mobile application reviews. In our immediate future work, we shall integrate this resource with RE methods for analysing and tracing semantic relatedness of software requirements. This in return, will aid in organising and grouping related system features described in requirements documents.The frame embeddings are publicly available at `https://doi.org/10.5281/zenodo.2605273`.

References

Alhoshan, W., Batista-navarro, R., and Zhao, L. (2018a). A framenet-based approach for annotating software requirements. In Torrent, T. T., Borin, L., and Baker, C. F., editors, *Proceedings of the Eleventh International Conference on Language Resources and Evaluation (LREC 2018)*, Paris, France. European Language Resources Association (ELRA).

Alhoshan, W., Batista-Navarro, R., and Zhao, L. (2018b). Towards a corpus of requirements documents enriched with semantic frame annotations. In *2018 IEEE 26th International Requirements Engineering Conference (RE)*, pages 428–431.

Alhoshan, W., Zhao, L., and Batista-Navarro, R. (2018c). Using semantic frames to identify related textual requirements: An initial validation. In *Proceedings of the 12th ACM/IEEE International Symposium on Empirical Software Engineering and Measurement*, ESEM '18, pages 58:1–58:2, New York, NY, USA. ACM.

Baker, C. F. (2017). Framenet: Frame semantic annotation in practice. In *Handbook of Linguistic Annotation*, pages 771–811. Springer.

Baker, C. F., Fillmore, C. J., and Lowe, J. B. (1998). The berkeley framenet project. In *Proceedings of the 17th international conference on Computational linguistics-Volume 1*, pages 86–90. Association for Computational Linguistics.

Bengio, Y., Ducharme, R., Vincent, P., and Janvin, C. (2003). A neural probabilistic language model. *J. Mach. Learn. Res.*, 3:1137–1155.

Dalpiaz, F., Ferrari, A., Franch, X., and Palomares, C. (2018). Natural language processing for requirements engineering: The best is yet to come. *IEEE Software*, 35(5):115–119.

Efstathiou, V., Chatzilenas, C., and Spinellis, D. (2018). Word embeddings for the software engineering domain. In *Proceedings of the 15th International Conference on Mining Software Repositories*, pages 38–41. ACM.

Fernández, D. M., Wagner, S., Kalinowski, M., Felderer, M., Mafra, P., Vetrò, A., Conte, T., Christiansson, M.-T., Greer, D., Lassenius, C., et al. (2017). Naming the pain in requirements engineering. *Empirical software engineering*, 22(5):2298–2338.

Ferrari, A., DellOrletta, F., Esuli, A., Gervasi, V., and Gnesi, S. (2017). Natural language requirements processing: a 4d vision. *IEEE Software*, (6):28–35.

Fillmore, C. J. (1976). Frame semantics and the nature of language. *Annals of the New York Academy of Sciences*, 280(1):20–32.

Fu, R., Guo, J., Qin, B., Che, W., Wang, H., and Liu, T. (2014). Learning semantic hierarchies via word embeddings. In *Proceedings of the 52nd Annual Meeting of the Association for Computational Linguistics (Volume 1: Long Papers)*, volume 1, pages 1199–1209.

Harris, Z. S. (1954). Distributional structure. *¡i¿WORD¡/i¿*, 10(2-3):146–162.

Hull, E., Jackson, K., and Dick, J. (2017). *Requirmenets Engineering*. Springer, London.

Jozefowicz, R., Vinyals, O., Schuster, M., Shazeer, N., and Wu, Y. (2016). Exploring the limits of language modeling. *arXiv preprint arXiv:1602.02410*.

Mahmoud, A. and Niu, N. (2015). On the role of semantics in automated requirements tracing. *Requir. Eng.*, 20(3):281–300.

Mikolov, T., Chen, K., Corrado, G., and Dean, J. (2013). Efficient estimation of word representations in vector space. *arXiv preprint arXiv:1301.3781*.

Sikos, J. and Padó, S. (2018). Using embeddings to compare framenet frames across languages. In *Proceedings of the First Workshop on Linguistic Resources for Natural Language Processing*, pages 91–101.

R-grams: Unsupervised Learning of Semantic Units

Ariel Ekgren[†]
RISE
ariel.ekgren@gmail.se

Amaru Cuba Gyllensten[†]
RISE
amaru.cuba.gyllensten@ri.se

Magnus Sahlgren
RISE
magnus.sahlgren@ri.se

Abstract

This paper investigates data-driven segmentation using Re-Pair or Byte Pair Encoding-techniques. In contrast to previous work which has primarily been focused on subword units for machine translation, we are interested in the general properties of such segments above the word level. We call these segments r-grams, and discuss their properties and the effect they have on the token frequency distribution. The proposed approach is evaluated by demonstrating its viability in embedding techniques, both in monolingual and multilingual test settings. We also provide a number of qualitative examples of the proposed methodology, demonstrating its viability as a language-invariant segmentation procedure.

1 Introduction

Natural Language Processing (NLP) requires data to be segmented into units. These units are normally called *words*, which in itself is a somewhat vague and controversial concept (Haspelmath, 2011) that is often operationalized as meaning something like "white-space (and punctuation) delimited string of characters". Of course, some languages do not use white-space delimiters, such as Chinese and Thai, which have context-dependent notions of what constitute words without special symbols dedicated to segmentation. As an example, the sequence 我喜欢新西兰花 can be segmented (correctly) in two different ways (Badino, 2004):

我/ 喜欢/ 新/ 西兰花
I like fresh broccoli
我/ 喜欢/ 新西兰/ 花
I like New Zealand flowers

Even for white-space segmenting languages, it is seldom as simple as merely using white-space delimited strings of characters as atomic units. As one example, morphologically sparse languages such as English rely to a large extent on word order to encode grammar, which means that such languages often form lexical multi-word units, which by all accounts function as atomic units on the same level as white-space delimited words. As an example, "white house" and "rock and roll" are both distinct semantic concepts that it would be beneficial to include as atomic units in an NLP application.

Of course, atomic units of language can also exist *below* the level of white-space delimited strings of characters. In linguistics, *morphemes* are defined as the atomic units of language. For synthetic languages such as Turkish, Finnish, or Greenlandic, where grammatical relations are encoded by morphology rather than word order, there can be a possibly large number of morphemes within one single white-space delimited string of characters. The canonical example in this case tends to be Western Greenlandic, which is a polysynthetic language that produces notoriously long white-space delimited string of characters. As an example, the string "tusaanngitsuusaartuaannarsinnaanngivipputit" consists of 9 different morphemes ("hear"|neg.|intrans.participle|"pretend"|"all the time"|"can"|neg.|"really"|2nd.sng.indicat.) and

[†]These authors contributed equally to the work.

means "you simply cannot pretend not to be hearing all the time". One white-space delimited string of characters in Western Greenlandic, eleven in English.

Similarly, compounding languages such as Swedish can form productive compounds, where a potentially large number of words (and morphemes) are compounded into one single white-space delimited string of characters. As an example, the string "forskningsinformationsförsörjningssystemet" is a compound of the words for research information supply system.

The arbitrariness of segmenting units based on white space becomes especially clear when considering translations between languages. As one example, the concept of a "knife sharpener" is realized as two white-space delimited strings of characters in English, one in Swedish ("knivslip"), and three in Spanish ("afilador de cuchillo").

Segmentation is thus as non-trivial as it is foundational for NLP. Consequently, there exists a large body of work on segmentation algorithms (often driven by the need for segmenting languages other than English). Examples include Webster and Kit (1992); Chen and Liu (1992); Saffran et al. (1996); Beeferman et al. (1999); Kiss and Strunk (2006); Huang et al. (2007). Related areas (from the perspective of segmentation) such as multiword expressions and morphological normalization also have a rich literature of prior art. For multiword expressions, see e.g. Sag et al. (2002); Baldwin and Kim (2010); Constant et al. (2017), and for morphological normalization see e.g. Porter (1980); Koskenniemi (1996); Yamashita and Matsumoto (2000).

In recent years, interest have begun to shift towards the use of *character-level* techniques, which bypass the problem of segmentation by simply operating on the raw character sequence. Much of this work is driven by research on deep learning, and techniques inspired by neural language models (Sutskever et al., 2011; Kim et al., 2016). In theory, such models can learn task-specific segmentations of the input that are optimal for solving whatever task the network is trained to perform.

The approach presented in this paper is inspired by character-level modeling, but in contrast to such techniques we seek a *task-independent* and *objective* segmentation of text. Our work is motivated by the idea that *if* there exists an optimal and language-invariant segmentation of text, it should be based on statistical properties of language rather than heuristics. We argue that such a segmentation exists, and introduce a novel type of data-driven segmented unit: the *recursion-gram* or *r-gram* in short. The name is inspired by the n-gram introduced by Shannon (1948), who used it to explore language modeling in the context of information entropy, which was also introduced in the same paper. Our approach is inspired by information theoretic concerns.

In the applications where r-grams can be used, it replaces segmentation but not necessarily normalization. R-grams capture a range of semantic units from morphemes (or more generally, parts of words) to words to compounds to multi-word units, all based on simple frequency statistics. In this paper, we demonstrate an algorithm for computing one type of r-grams, and discuss novel observations and characteristics of the statistical distribution of natural language. We then demonstrate how r-grams can be used as basic building blocks in embeddings, and evaluate the resulting embeddings using both monolingual and multilingual test sets. We conclude the paper with some directions for future research.

2 R-grams and compression algorithms

Given a sequence over a finite alphabet, an r-gram is a variable length subsequence, derived by a set of well defined statistical rules, segmenting the original sequence into a set of subsequences.

2.1 A first class of r-grams

The fundamental idea of r-grams is deceptively simple. Given a sequence of discrete symbols sampled from a finite alphabet, find *the most common pair* of adjacent symbols and *replace* all instances of the pair with instances of a new single symbol, extending the alphabet by one, repeat until no more pairs can be found or some other criterion is fulfilled.

Iteration	Sequence	Alphabet	Replacement
0	$s =< \beta, \beta, \beta, \alpha, \beta, \beta, \beta, \alpha, \beta, \beta, \beta >$	$A = \alpha, \beta$	$< \beta, \beta > \rightarrow \gamma$
1	$s =< \gamma, \beta, \alpha, \gamma, \beta, \alpha, \gamma, \beta >$	$A = \alpha, \beta, \gamma$	$< \gamma, \beta > \rightarrow \delta$
2	$s =< \delta, \alpha, \delta, \alpha, \delta >$	$A = \alpha, \beta, \gamma, \delta$	

Table 1: Procedure to derive r-grams.

Table 1 illustrates an example where we have a sequence S and an alphabet A. We show the first two iterations of the algorithm, at each step identifying the most common pair in the sequence and replacing it by a new symbol. Two new symbols γ and δ are introduced. We observe a hierarchical structure where δ contains γ which in turn contains symbols from the original alphabet. δ can thus be expanded into three elements from the original alphabet $\delta = (\beta, \beta, \beta)$. The observant reader might notice that there are some cases that require additional definitions. If two pairs overlap, as in the original sequence in the example, a rule for which pair to replace first has to be defined. In this example the rule was that the first from left to right observed pair is replaced. Another case is when there are more than one alternative for the most common pair, when the pairs has an equal amount of observations, then a rule on which pair to prioritize has to be defined. In the example above two r-grams were created: $\gamma =< \beta, \beta >$ and $\delta =< \beta, \beta, \beta >$.

If n iterations of this procedure are performed on a sequence, the sequence is compressed, but the alphabet is expanded. Given that the compression of the sequence is larger than the expansion of the alphabet, we end up with a more compact representation of the underlying sequence. This exact procedure turns out to be an excellent compression algorithm named re-pair in the family of dictionary-based compression (Larsson and Moffat, 2000). A remarkable property of this procedure is that, if the sequence is generated by an ergodic process, the segmented sequence becomes asymptotically Markov as the procedure is continually applied (Benedetto et al., 2006).

A close relative to the re-pair algorithm is Byte Pair Encoding (BPE) (Gage, 1994), first used in the context of segmentation by Schuster and Nakajima (2012) and recently popularized in within deep learning by Sennrich et al. (2016). The segmentation method has primarily been used for finding subword units for later processing in recurrent neural networks, e.g. Wu et al. (2016) Sennrich et al. (2016).

Published libraries for Byte Pair Encoding as segmentation exists in the form of, e.g. SentencePiece Kudo and Richardson (2018), and the resulting segments are commonly referred to as either "sentencepieces" or "wordpieces", the latter stressing their use as *sub*word units. Functionally, the difference between such segmentation procedures and the r-gram algorithm is small, if at all existent. Crucially, however, we are interested in the *properties* of the segmented units (which we call r-grams) and the grammar they form, rather than their use as a preprocessing step.

2.2 Implementation details

The naive r-gram algorithm runs in quadratic time relative to the sequence length: find the most common pair in linear time, merge it, and repeat the process. This is prohibitively expensive. Thankfully there exists algorithms (namely re-pair and BPE) that recalculates the pair-frequencies in an efficient way, resulting in linear time algorithms. We have implemented a slightly modified version of the re-pair algorithm laid out in Larsson and Moffat (2000) that allows for other stopping criteria and accounts for document and sentence boundaries:

Stopping criterion. We define two stopping criteria for the merges of the r-grams, which we simply call minimum frequency and maximum vocabulary. The minimum frequency criterion states that a new r-gram can be merged if its frequency exceeds the minimum frequency threshold, and the maximum vocabulary criterion simple states that new r-grams can be merged as long as the size of the vocabulary does not exceed the maximum vocabulary threshold.

Sequences boundaries. In natural language there are segmentations that signal a new local context such as sentence, paragraph or document boundaries. We generalize our statistics and alphabet collection over these boundaries but we do not create r-grams that overlap them.

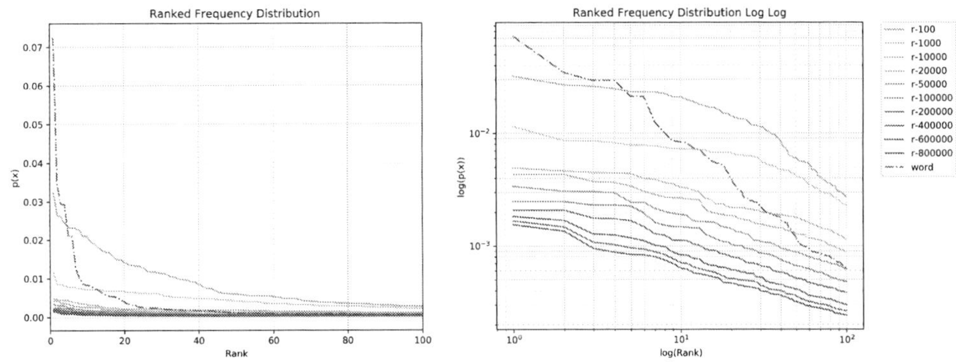

Figure 1: Ranked word and r-gram frequency distribution for the first hundred items in a subset of English Wikipedia.

The result of the re-pair compression algorithm on sequence S is (**1**) a mapping from r-grams to their constituent parts (e.g. $\gamma \rightarrow \langle \beta, \beta \rangle$ from example 1) and (**2**) a compressed sequence S_c of the original sequence S, where S_c is a sequence of r-grams rather than symbols from the original alphabet. By applying the mapping recursively down to the terminal symbols, the original sequence can be restored. When using r-grams as a segmentation technique, the sequence S_c is taken to be a segmentation of S.

3 Frequency distribution of data

It is a well-known fact that the vocabulary of natural languages as segmented by traditional approaches follow a Zipfian distribution (Zipf, 1932). It is also a well-known fact that the majority of the frequency spectrum of traditionally segmented natural language is comprised of a small number of very high-frequent items, which are normally referred to as *stop words*. These high-frequent items are normally viewed as semantically vacuous, and are therefore generally not included in NLP applications. This practice has been around since the 1950s, when Hans Peter Luhn connected the "resolving power" of words in language to their frequency distribution (Luhn, 1958). Current methods in NLP still use basically the same type of algorithmic compensation for the power law distribution of word tokens in written text, whether it is the use of inverse document frequency in document processing applications, or subsampling (Mikolov et al., 2013), mutual information (Church and Hanks, 1990), or incremental frequency weighting (Sahlgren et al., 2016) in word embeddings. There is even debate whether the Zipfian distribution is an inherent language-specific feature or an emergent phenomenon sprung from the process of drawing and counting various-length character sequences from a finite alphabet (Piantadosi, 2014).

From an information theoretic and information entropy perspective, a uniform distribution carries the most surprise (Shannon, 1948) and thus also the most information. The Zipfian distribution belongs to the power law family and is highly non-uniform. Keeping both the practice of throwing away stop words and the information entropy perspective in mind, there is reason to believe that there exists more informative segmentations than word level segmentation for natural language.

Figure 1 shows the ranked frequency distributions for the 100 most high-frequent words and r-grams in a subset of English Wikipedia. The r-grams are computed over an increasing number of iterations (the r parameter), and the figure clearly shows how the frequency distribution is flattened as the number of iterations of the r-gram algorithm is increased. This is a natural consequence of the algorithm, since it finds common elements and reforges some of them into new elements, reducing the frequency of common elements. In of itself this observation does not hold much value, but inspecting the r-grams created it seems that they capture semantic regularities such as morphemes, words and multi word units. Table 2 demonstrates the effect of applying the algorithm to a 735MB sample text drawn from English Wikipedia. Note that after 100 iterations, the algorithm has formed the copula ("is") and a determiner

Merges	Text
10	r a n n e b er g er _ (b o r n _ 1 9 4 9) _ i s _a _ f o r m er _ u
100	r an n e b er g er_ (b or n _ 19 4 9) _ is _a_ for m er_ un it ed_
1000	ran ne ber g er_ (born _ 194 9) _is_a_ form er_ united_stat es _am
20000	ran ne berg er_(born_ 1949)_is_a_former_ united_states _ambassador
100000	ran ne berg er_(born_ 1949)_is_a_former_ united_states _ambassador_t
400000	ran neberg er_(born_ 1949)_is_a_former_ united_states_ambassador_to_

Table 2: Textual example of r-grams being merged from English Wikipedia

("a"). After 1000 iterations, it has collapsed these into a common unit ("is a") as well as the word "born" and the beginning of the collocation "united states". After 400 000 iterations, the algorithm has learned several long sequences, such as "is a former" and "united states ambassador to".

Note that this has been learned from the statistics of the sequence alone, with all characters being treated as equal with no specific rules for whitespace or other special characters, with the exception for sequence separators such as newline. The important thing to note is that the r-gram algorithm learns units that would normally be discarded in NLP applications, since they contain (or, in the extreme case, consist entirely of) stop words. As an example, the phrase "has yet to be" constitutes a semantically useful unit that would be completely discarded when using standard stop word filtering.

4 Experiments

4.1 R-grams in word embeddings

The domain of NLP that focuses specifically on the *semantics* of units of language is called *distributional semantics*, where semantics is modeled using *distributional vectors* or *word embeddings*. Word embeddings encode semantic similarity by minimizing distance between vectors in a latent space, which is defined by co-occurrence information. Many methods for creating word embeddings have been proposed (Turney and Pantel, 2010). Segmentation, as a preprocessing step, has a significant impact on the quality of word embeddings. The standard procedure is to simply rely on the white-space heuristic, and to remove all punctuation. This invariably leads to conflation of collocations in the distributional representations, and to problems with out of vocabulary items.

To counter such problems, one may use preprocessing techniques to detect significant multiword expressions (Mikolov et al., 2013) and morphological normalization (Bullinaria and Levy, 2012), or one may try to incorporate string similarity into the distributional representation (Bojanowski et al., 2017), or detect collocations directly from the vector properties (Sahlgren et al., 2016).

A radically different approach, suggested by Oshikiri (2017), is to produce embeddings for a subset of all possible character n-grams. This alleviates the need for preprocessing completely, but requires delimiting the subset with respect to the size of the n-grams, and their frequency of occurrence. Schütze (2017) also operates of character n-grams, but uses a random segmentation of the data. R-grams is similar in spirit to these previous approaches, but in contrast to the parameters required by Oshikiri (2017), r-grams put no restrictions on the size of the units, or on their frequencies (except for the minimum frequency stopping criterion).

In order to demonstrate the applicability of r-grams for building word embeddings, we use a 735MB[1] subset of English Wikipedia for this experiment. The only preprocessing used before creating r-grams is lowercasing, for embeddings we also substitute numbers $0-9$ with N and remove leading and trailing whitespaces from the r-grams. When building embeddings, we use skipgram with subword units (Bojanowski et al., 2017), a window size of 2, and evaluate the models on standard *single word* English embedding benchmarks[2]. It is worth noting that the skipgram model uses subsampling of common

[1]The quality of the r-grams seem to correlate strongly to the amount of data they are derived from, more data equals better semantic representations. Our selected data size was dependent on the available RAM on the machine used for experiments.

[2]https://github.com/kudkudak/word-embeddings-benchmarks

Test	r-grams	words	Test	r-grams	words
AP	0.58	0.56	RW	0.31	0.39
BLESS	0.59	0.75	SimLex999	0.36	0.39
Battig	0.36	0.40	WS353	0.60	0.67
ESSLI_1a	0.73	0.75	WS353R	0.53	0.61
ESSLI_2b	0.77	0.80	WS353S	0.68	0.70
ESSLI_2c	0.62	0.71	Google	0.32	0.33
MEN	0.68	0.73	MSR	0.39	0.39
MTurk	0.64	0.67	SemEval2012_2	0.18	0.21
RG65	0.66	0.73			

Table 3: Comparison of word embeddings benchmarks using r-grams and words.

#	**'back to the future'**	Cos	#	**'has yet to be'**	Cos
1.	'who framed roger rabbit'	0.78	1.	'has not been'	0.69
2.	'dr. no'	0.77	2.	'has not yet been'	0.68
3.	'show boat'	0.76	3.	'was never'	0.59
4.	'nightmare on elm street'	0.75	4.	'had not been'	0.59
5.	'apocalypse now'	0.75	5.	'has never been'	0.59
#	**'counterintelligence'**	Cos	#	**'psychology'**	Cos
1.	'counterterrorism'	0.56	1.	'sociology'	0.69
2.	'intelligence community'	0.55	2.	'social psychology'	0.66
3.	'counter-terrorism'	0.54	3.	'anthropology'	0.65
4.	'intelligence'	0.52	4.	'political theory'	0.64
5.	'advanced research project'	0.51	5.	'political science'	0.62

Table 4: Examples of the 5 nearest neighbors to four different targets in the r-gram embedding.

words, which is an optimization introduced to compensate for the power law distribution in common vocabularies. Also, the skipgram model controls for collocations by dampening the impact of frequent collocations. This implies that the skipgram model might not be the optimal choice for creating embeddings from data driven segmentation. It was, however, the best performing model of those we tried during initial testing.

Table 3 shows the results of the embeddings produced using r-gram segmented data in comparison with whitespace segmented data. Note that the benchmark results in general are almost as good for the r-gram embedding as they are for the word embedding. In particular the analogy tests (Google and MSR) show no, or negligible, difference in the results between the r-gram embedding and the word embedding. This is remarkable, since the r-grams have been learned directly from the character sequence, with no preconceptions of what constitutes viable semantic units. Taken by themselves, the scores for the r-gram embedding are competitive, and demonstrate the viability of the approach.

The benchmarks used in Table 3 only include single words. However, the r-grams range from parts of words to multiword expressions, strictly derived from the statistical distribution of the elements in the original sequence. In order to illustrate the qualitative properties of the r-gram embedding, Table 4 show examples of the 10 nearest neighbors to a selected set of r-grams. Note that the r-grams may include punctuation as in "dr. no" and "a hard day's", and that the embedding includes phrases such as "has yet to be" (and all its neighbors) that would normally have been filtered out by stop word removal. The qualitative examples use the skipgram model without subword information.

4.2 R-grams as a language agnostic segmentation technique

To test whether or not r-gram segmentation is a viable language-agnostic segmentation technique we evaluate r-gram embeddings on the analogy test sets in (Grave et al., 2018). These consist of (unbalanced) analogy tests for Czech, German, English, Spanish, Finnish, French, Hindi, Italian, Polish, Portuguese, and Chinese. For each language, we use a 750MB sample of Wikipedia, r-gram segmented with a stopping criteria of either *minimum frequency* of 4 or *maximum vocabulary* of 800000. As an additional preprocessing step we remove whitespace characters from the ends of r-grams: 'example_' → 'example'[3] The resulting, slightly modified, r-gram segmentation is then used to train r-gram embeddings using the skipgram model with subword units, as described in the previous subsection.

Despite the large variation across languages, the results in Table 5 demonstrate that r-gram segmentation does indeed constitute a viable language-agnostic segmentation technique, albeit with poorer performance in the analogy tasks compared to regular segmentation.

		CS	DE	ES	FI	FR	HI	IT	PL	PT	ZH	Average
Score	r-gram	0.60	0.25	0.35	0.09	0.15	0.10	0.36	0.24	0.13	0.30	0.26
	baseline	0.63	0.61	0.57	0.36	0.64	0.11	0.56	0.53	0.54	0.60	0.51
Coverage	r-gram	0.66	0.54	0.64	0.85	0.67	0.40	0.52	0.38	0.61	0.96	0.62
	baseline	0.77	0.79	0.94	0.95	0.88	0.71	0.81	0.70	0.79	1.00	0.83

Table 5: R-gram and baseline performance and coverage on the word analogy tasks. The baseline is taken from Grave et al. (2018)

Part of the explanation for the relatively poor performance both here and the tests in the previous section is that the r-gram segmentation technique construct many near synonymous tokens. Table 6 shows an example of this for the analogy query "Great Britain is to the United States as Pound is to ? " in Finnish. The correct term according to the evaluation data set is 'dollari', which is not in the top ten candidates. However, 'yhdysvaltain dollaria' (U.S. Dollar), is the second candidate. Dually, the top candidate is 'punt', which is a subword unit of 'punta', 'puntaa', 'puntin' et.c. We believe both of these types of near synonymous words, and their relative abundance in the r-gram vocabulary, has a detrimental effect on the word-based evaluation benchmarks.

Going into a more qualitative view of what is represented by the r-gram embeddings in different languages, Table 7 shows the nearest neighbors to two different acronyms ("vw" and "kgb") in 6 different languages. The column marked # indicates rank of the neighbor (i.e. 1 means the closest neighbor, and 7 means the seventh neighbor). The examples in Table 7 demonstrate not only that the r-gram segmentation produces useful semantic units in all languages used in these experiments, but also that they constitute viable data for building embeddings; associated r-grams to "vw" are terms such as "volkswagen" and other automobile-related multiword units. The same applies to the neighbors of "kgb"; neighbors are terms related to the secret police and security services. Again, note that all these terms were found by the unsupervised r-gram process.

The examples in Table 7 where chosen with the intent to highlight how short r-grams can be viewed as semantically similar neighbors to longer r-grams. Next we turn to a demonstration of how the r-gram embeddings can be mapped across languages using a recently proposed unsupervised projection model (MUSE) (Lample et al., 2018). Their method leverages adversarial training to learn a linear mapping from a source to a target space, aligning embeddings trained on separate data allowing us to translate by finding similar vectors between the embeddings. Table 8 demonstrates examples of translation between German and Spanish. In the first case we see how a single word in German ("kürzer", eng. "shorter") is mapped to relevant multiword units in Spanish. Note that the only difference between the first and second Spanish neighbor is the comma at the end. In the second example we see how a multiword unit in Spanish ("las ideas", eng. "the ideas") is mapped to relevant single word units in German.

5 Conclusions

The main contribution of this paper is its novel perspective on segmentation as a statistical process operating on the raw character sequence. We believe that the application of this general process is not limited to language, but that it is generally applicable to compressible sequences of categorical data in

[3]This step — while not strictly necessary — was performed to better match the terms in the analogy tests.

#	**'punta' − 'englanti' + 'yhdysvallat'**	Cos	Translation
1.	'punt'	0.53	'Pound'
2.	'yhdysvaltain dollaria'	0.50	'U.S. Dollar'
3.	'kun yhdysvallat'	0.49	'When United States'
4.	'yhdysvaltain dollari'	0.48	'U.S. Dollar'
5.	'yhdysvaltain dollarin'	0.47	'U.S. Dollar'

Table 6: Table showing analogy query candidates for finnish. The correct term according to the evaluation data set is 'dollari' which is only found as part of larger r-grams in the returned candidates.

Lang.	#	**'vw'**
Spanish	1.	'volkswagen passat'
German	1.	'volkswagen'
Czech	1.	'koncernu volkswagen'
Finnish	1.	'volkswagen golf'
French	7.	'volkswagen'
Polish	1.	'volkswagen'

Lang.	#	**'kgb'**
Spanish	4.	'policía secreta'
German	1.	'geheimdienstes'
Czech	2.	'státní bezpečnosti'
Finnish	8.	'yhdysvaltain keskustiedustelupalvelu'
French	8.	'service de renseignement'
Polish	5.	'głównego zarządu bezpieczeństwa państwowego'

Table 7: Examples of nearest neighbors in the r-gram embeddings in different languages to two different acronyms.

order to find units and hierarchies. The fact that an r-gram is generated from a global context compression algorithm, and is also interpretable, is an interesting observation from the perspective of viewing AI as a compression problem (Mahoney, 1999; Legg and Hutter, 2007), which also suggests interesting directions for future work.

The substitution of the most common pair of types with a new type could be thought of as forming rules in a grammar. A lot of work has been done on inferring the smallest possible grammar (which turns out to be an NP complete problem (Charikar et al., 2005)), as well as efficient grammar construction from local contexts (Nevill-Manning and Witten, 1997). The r-gram grammar (or graph) constitutes a very different type of grammar that contains both context, frequent collocations and natural subword units. It would be interesting to further investigate potential applications of this grammar; one interesting question is how the grammars differ between languages and in what ways they can be exploited in translation tasks, another very interesting possibility is to build embeddings directly on the grammar, since it records all necessary contextual information. Preliminary work indicates that generating embeddings directly from the r-gram grammar is a promising path going forward.

German to Spanish		Spanish to German	
'kürzer'	('shorter')	**'las ideas'**	('the ideas')
'más corto'	('shorter')	'überzeugungen'	('convictions')
'más corto,'	('shorter')	'tendenzen'	('trends')
'mucho más larg'	('much more larg(e)')	'gedankengänge'	('thought processes')
'muy corto'	('very short')	'ideologien'	('ideologies')
'más cortos'	('shorter')	'moralvorstellungen'	('moral values')

Table 8: Examples of crosslingual nearest neighbors using r-gram embeddings mapped with the MUSE algorithm. Words in parenthesis are English translation for the benefit of the reader.

References

Leonardo Badino. 2004. Chinese text word-segmentation considering semantic links among sentences. In *Proceedings of Interspeech.*

Timothy Baldwin and Su Nam Kim. 2010. Multiword expressions. In *Handbook of Natural Language Processing*, pages 267–292. Chapman and Hall/CRC.

Doug Beeferman, Adam Berger, and John Lafferty. 1999. Statistical models for text segmentation. *Machine Learning*, 34(1):177–210.

Dario Benedetto, Emanuele Caglioti, and Davide Gabrielli. 2006. Non-sequential recursive pair substitution: some rigorous results. *Journal of Statistical Mechanics: Theory and Experiment*, 2006(09):P09011.

Piotr Bojanowski, Edouard Grave, Armand Joulin, and Tomas Mikolov. 2017. Enriching word vectors with subword information. *Transactions of the Association for Computational Linguistics*, 5:135–146.

John Bullinaria and Joseph P. Levy. 2012. Extracting semantic representations from word co-occurrence statistics: stop-lists, stemming, and svd. *Behavior Research Methods*, 44:890–907.

Moses Charikar, Eric Lehman, Ding Liu, Rina Panigrahy, Manoj Prabhakaran, Amit Sahai, and Abhi Shelat. 2005. The smallest grammar problem. *IEEE Transactions on Information Theory*, 51(7):2554–2576.

Keh-Jiann Chen and Shing-Huan Liu. 1992. Word identification for mandarin chinese sentences. In *Proceedings of the COLING*, pages 101–107.

Kenneth Ward Church and Patrick Hanks. 1990. Word association norms, mutual information, and lexicography. *Computational Linguistics*, 16(1):22–29.

Mathieu Constant, Gülşen Eryiğit, Johanna Monti, Lonneke van der Plas, Carlos Ramisch, Michael Rosner, and Amalia Todirascu. 2017. Multiword expression processing: A survey. *Computational Linguistics*, 43(4):837–892.

Philip Gage. 1994. A new algorithm for data compression. *C Users J.*, 12(2):23–38.

Edouard Grave, Piotr Bojanowski, Prakhar Gupta, Armand Joulin, and Tomas Mikolov. 2018. Learning word vectors for 157 languages. In *Proceedings of LREC.*

M. Haspelmath. 2011. The indeterminacy of word segmentation and the nature of morphology and syntax. *Folia Linguistica*, 45(1):31–80.

Chu-Ren Huang, Petr Šimon, Shu-Kai Hsieh, and Laurent Prévot. 2007. Rethinking chinese word segmentation: Tokenization, character classification, or wordbreak identification. In *Proceedings of ACL*, pages 69–72.

Yoon Kim, Yacine Jernite, David Sontag, and Alexander M. Rush. 2016. Character-aware neural language models. In *Proceedings of AAAI*, pages 2741–2749.

Tibor Kiss and Jan Strunk. 2006. Unsupervised multilingual sentence boundary detection. *Computational Linguistics*, 32(4):485–525.

Kimmo Koskenniemi. 1996. Finite state morphology in information retrieval. *Natural Language Engineering*, 2.

Taku Kudo and John Richardson. 2018. Sentencepiece: A simple and language independent subword tokenizer and detokenizer for neural text processing. In *Proceedings of the 2018 Conference on Empirical Methods in Natural Language Processing: System Demonstrations*, pages 66–71.

Guillaume Lample, Alexis Conneau, Ludovic Denoyer, and Marc'Aurelio Ranzato. 2018. Unsupervised machine translation using monolingual corpora only. In *Proceedings of ICLR*.

N Jesper Larsson and Alistair Moffat. 2000. Off-line dictionary-based compression. *Proceedings of the IEEE*, 88(11):1722–1732.

Shane Legg and Marcus Hutter. 2007. Universal intelligence: A definition of machine intelligence. *Minds and Machines*, 17(4):391–444.

Hans Peter Luhn. 1958. The automatic creation of literature abstracts. *IBM Journal of research and development*, 2(2):159–165.

Matthew V Mahoney. 1999. Text compression as a test for artificial intelligence. In *AAAI/IAAI*, page 970.

Tomas Mikolov, Ilya Sutskever, Kai Chen, Greg S Corrado, and Jeff Dean. 2013. Distributed representations of words and phrases and their compositionality. In *Proceedings of NIPS*, pages 3111–3119.

Craig G Nevill-Manning and Ian H Witten. 1997. Identifying hierarchical structure in sequences: A linear-time algorithm. *Journal of Artificial Intelligence Research*, 7:67–82.

Takamasa Oshikiri. 2017. Segmentation-free word embedding for unsegmented languages. In *Proceedings of EMNLP*, pages 767–772.

Steven T Piantadosi. 2014. Zipf's word frequency law in natural language: A critical review and future directions. *Psychonomic bulletin & review*, 21(5):1112–1130.

Martin F Porter. 1980. An algorithm for suffix stripping. *Program*, 14(3):130–137.

Jenny R Saffran, Elissa L Newport, and Richard N Aslin. 1996. Word segmentation: The role of distributional cues. *Journal of memory and language*, 35(4):606–621.

Ivan A Sag, Timothy Baldwin, Francis Bond, Ann Copestake, and Dan Flickinger. 2002. Multiword expressions: A pain in the neck for nlp. In *Proceedings of CICLing*, pages 1–15.

Magnus Sahlgren, Amaru Cuba Gyllensten, Fredrik Espinoza, Ola Hamfors, Anders Holst, Jussi Karlgren, Fredrik Olsson, Per Persson, and Akshay Viswanathan. 2016. The Gavagai Living Lexicon. In *Proceedings of LREC*.

Mike Schuster and Kaisuke Nakajima. 2012. Japanese and korean voice search. In *ICASSP*, pages 5149–5152.

Hinrich Schütze. 2017. Nonsymbolic text representation. In *Proceedings of EACL*, pages 785–796.

Rico Sennrich, Barry Haddow, and Alexandra Birch. 2016. Neural machine translation of rare words with subword units. In *Proceedings of ACL*, pages 1715–1725.

Claude E. Shannon. 1948. A mathematical theory of communication. *Bell System Technical Journal*, 27(3):379–423.

Ilya Sutskever, James Martens, and Geoffrey Hinton. 2011. Generating text with recurrent neural networks. In *Proceedings of ICML*, pages 1017–1024.

Peter D Turney and Patrick Pantel. 2010. From frequency to meaning: Vector space models of semantics. *Journal of artificial intelligence research*, 37:141–188.

Jonathan J. Webster and Chunyu Kit. 1992. Tokenization as the initial phase in nlp. In *Proceedings of COLING*, pages 1106–1110.

Yonghui Wu, Mike Schuster, Zhifeng Chen, Quoc V Le, Mohammad Norouzi, Wolfgang Macherey, Maxim Krikun, Yuan Cao, Qin Gao, Klaus Macherey, et al. 2016. Google's neural machine translation system: Bridging the gap between human and machine translation. *arXiv preprint arXiv:1609.08144*.

Tatsuo Yamashita and Yuji Matsumoto. 2000. Language independent morphological analysis. In *Proceedings of ANLC*, pages 232–238.

G. K. Zipf. 1932. *Selective Studies and the Principle of Relative Frequency in Language*. Harvard University Press.